WHO'S AFRAID
OF
LIBERAL EDUCATION?

QUI A PEUR
DE
L'ÉDUCATION GÉNÉRALE?

WHO'S AFRAID OF LIBERAL EDUCATION?

Proceedings
of the National Conference
organized by the Social Science Federation of Canada
and held in Ottawa, Ontario
September 30th — October 1st, 1988.

Edited by Caroline Andrew and Steen B. Esbensen

QUI A PEUR DE L'ÉDUCATION GÉNÉRALE?

Communications présentées au colloque national
organisé par la Fédération canadienne des sciences sociales
et tenu à Ottawa (Ontario)
le 30 septembre et le 1er octobre 1988.

Textes réunis par Caroline Andrew et
Steen B. Esbensen

University of Ottawa Press
Ottawa • London • Paris

Les Presses de l'Université d'Ottawa
Ottawa • Paris • Londres

Canadian Cataloguing in Publication Data
Main entry under title:
Who's afraid of liberal education?
= Qui a peur de l'éducation générale?
Text in English and French.
Includes bibliographic references.
ISBN 0-7766-0276-4

1. Education, Humanistic — Canada — Congresses.
2. Education, Higher — Canada — Congresses.
3. Universities and colleges — Canada — Curricula — Congresses.
I. Andrew, Caroline, 1942-
II. Esbensen, Steen B.
III. Title.
IV. Title: Qui a peur de l'éducation générale?

LC1011.W56 1989   378'.012'0971   C89-090401-4E

Données de catalogage avant publication (Canada)
Vedette principale au titre:
Who's afraid of liberal education?
= Qui a peur de l'éducation générale?
Textes en anglais et en français.
Comprend des références bibliographiques.
ISBN 2-7766-0276-4

1. Éducation humaniste — Canada — Congrès.
2. Enseignement supérieur — Canada — Congrès.
3. Universités — Canada — Programmes d'études — Congrès.
I. Andrew, Caroline, 1942-
II. Esbensen, Steen B.
III. Titre
IV. Titre: Qui a peur de l'éducation générale?

LC1011.W56 1989   378'.012'0971   C89-090401-4F

Production / design: Jean-Paul Morisset
Cover / couverture: Communication graphique Gagnon-Bélanger
© University of Ottawa Press /
Les Presses de l'Université d'Ottawa
1989
Printed and bound in Canada / Imprimé et relié au Canada

CONTENTS / SOMMAIRE

FOREWORD

In 1988, the Social Science Federation chose to organize a conference on the theme "Who's Afraid of Liberal Education?" The title was chosen to provoke discussion and debate about the current nature and desired orientation of undergraduate education in Canada.

This question is not new and, indeed, the choice of this theme was influenced by the discussions held at the National Forum on Post-secondary Education, held in Saskatoon in October 1987. One of the conclusions emerging from the Forum was that there is an urgent need in Canada for better educated, highly qualified human resources. Recurrent themes in these discussions were the need for more adaptability, better communication skills and less specialization at the undergraduate level.

Other conferences and workshops, focusing on similar preoccupations, have been held recently in Quebec (Colloque de l'Université du Québec sur les orientations du premier cycle, octobre 1987). In addition, programmes have been set up and others are in the planning stages. And, to the south, the United States offers a vast array of programmes, reports and reflections on questions of liberal education, core curricula general studies and the more general question of the adaptation of the undergraduate programme to a changing society. These same preoccupations are emerging widely, as can be seen from the conclusions of a recent OECD Conference (Education and the Economy in a Changing Society, Paris, March 1988) :

FOREWORD

> To promote maximum flexibility and adaptability all young people need a broad base of transferable skills through a broad general initial education. (OECD Press Release, 18-3-1988).

Although this is a question of interest not only to the Social Sciences, it is clearly one of interest to the Social Sciences. In organizing the conference, the Social Science Federation of Canada wanted to indicate our interest in the question of the nature and direction of undergraduate education and our willingness to work with the broad university community in stimulating debate and in looking for solutions.

The intent of the conference was indeed to look for solutions. There has been wide discussion of the overall question of a liberal education but often it has been at a very general level. It was very much our hope that this conference would offer the chance to focus on concrete strategies for, and barriers to, change in the University curriculum. The intent was to focus on questions of how to bring about change. The title was deliberately chosen to focus on the strategies of implementation.

We are publishing the proceedings of the conference in order to pursue discussion of these questions. The proceedings are being published as they were presented, except that Gilles Paquet very kindly agreed to provide an introductionary chapter to the proceedings and, also very kindly, Michael Skolnik enlarged his substantial evaluation of the liberal education debate.

Caroline Andrew
Steen B. Esbensen

AVANT-PROPOS

En 1988, la Fédération canadienne des sciences sociale décida d'organiser une conférence dont le thème serait : "Qui a peur de l'éducation libérale?". Le titre de la conférence avait été choisi en vue de stimuler un débat sur la nature actuelle et les orientations éventuelles du curriculum de premier cycle au Canada.

Cette question en est une d'actualité, car le choix de ce thème découle en quelque sorte des discussions qui ont eu lieu dans le cadre du Forum national sur l'enseignement postsecondaire qui s'est tenu à Saskatoon au mois d'octobre 1987. Le besoin urgent de ressources humaines hautement qualifiées est une des conclusions importantes de cette rencontre nationale. La faculté d'adaptation, les compétences en communication et une moins grande spécialisation au niveau du premier cycle sont des thèmes qui sont revenus souvent au cours de forum.

D'autres conférences et ateliers portant sur cette question ont eu lieu au Québec (Colloque de l'Université du Québec sur les orientations du premier cycle, octobre 1987) et en Nouvelle-Écosse (Dalhousie Symposium on Undergraduate Education, March 1988). De surcroît, divers programmes ont été créés tandis que d'autres sont en train d'être mis sur pied dans de nombreuses universités. La question est aussi d'actualité chez nos voisins du Sud, où il existe à l'heure actuelle une vaste gamme de programmes et de nombreux rapports portant sur la question de l'éducation libérale, le curriculum de base et les études générales. La faculté d'adaptation du programme de premier cycle dans notre société en évolution est aussi vivement débattue. Ces mêmes préoccupations se manifestent de manière générale, comme nous le laissent entendre les conclusions tirées d'une conférence de l'OCDE (Education and the Economy in a Changing Society, Paris, mars 1988) :

> Afin d'assurer une grande souplesse et de favoriser la faculté d'adaptation, les jeunes doivent acquérir des compétences polyvalentes par le truchement d'un programme d'études générales. (Traduction libre.)

Bien que la question de l'éducation libérale ne soit pas propre aux sciences sociales, elle les intéresse au plus haut niveau. L'objet de notre conférence était de montrer l'intérêt que la Féderation canadienne des sciences sociales porte à la nature et aux orientations de l'éducation libérale, ainsi que notre volonté de collaborer avec la communauté universitaire en stimulant le débat et en cherchant des solutions.

Le but principal de la rencontre était en effet la recherche de solutions. Quoique la question de l'éducation libérale stimule de nombreuses discussions, celles-ci sont d'ordinaire très générales. Nous souhaitions que la conférence permette aux participants et aux participantes de faire le point sur les stratégies à employer et les obstacles à affronter dans le cadre de la réforme du curriculum de premier cycle. En choisissant le titre, nous voulions délibérément situer les discussions au niveau de la réalisation d'un nouveau curriculum.

Nous publions les actes de la conférence dans l'espoir qu'ils susciteront un débat. Les actes sont publiés tel quels mais nous y ajoutons un chapitre d'introduction que M. Gilles Paquet a aimablement accepté de rédiger. De surcroît, M. Michael Skolnik a accepté de préciser davantage son évaluation du débat entourant la question de l'éducation libérale.

Caroline Andrew
Steen B. Esbensen

ACKNOWLEDGEMENTS

This publication represents the proceedings of the national conference on the undergraduate curriculum organized by the Social Science Federation of Canada. Its theme was "Who's Afraid of Liberal Education?" The conference, which was held in Ottawa, September 30 — October 1, 1988, provided participants with an opportunity not only to hear about challenges, experiments and evaluations but also to engage actively in workshop discussions dealing with the barriers to and the strategies for formulating the content of a new curriculum for post-secondary education. This publication does not cover all the discussions which ensued in the workshops, it does however include the contributions of all the speakers. With these proceedings we hope that the heart of the conference will be able to spread and generate further reflection around the curriculum debate in post-secondary institutions in Canada.

We would like to thank the members of the conference organizing committee who assisted in and influenced the direction of the conference : Jane Gaskell, Paule Leduc, Camille Limoges, Todd Smith, Susan Mann Trofimenkoff, Miles Wisenthal, Christian Pouyez and Carol Bujeau.

We also wish to thank the staff of the Federation; Sylvie Provost, Geneviève Régimbald and Carol Bujeau for their careful attention to the details of the conference accommodations and physical logistics.

ACKNOWLEDGEMENTS

We gratefully acknowledge the Secretary of State for its generous financial assistance to the conference.

We also acknowledge a debt of gratitude to the many organizations and colleagues who were supportive of the idea of the conference and actively participated in the workshop disccusions and reported on the conference to their respective organizations. Notably we thank the AUCC and the CAUT for covering the conference in their respective publications.

In closing we wish particularly to underline our thanks to the former Executive Director of the Federation, Christian Pouyez, who had the foresight to pursue the conference theme and help to make it the success that it was.

REMERCIEMENTS

Nous sommes heureux de vous présenter les actes de la conférence nationale sur le nouveau curriculum de premier cycle organisée par la Fédération canadienne des sciences sociales. La conférence, intitulée "Qui a peur de l'éducation générale?", s'est tenue à Ottawa du 30 septembre au 1er octobre 1988. La rencontre a permis aux participants et aux participantes de discuter de diverses expériences tentées dans les universités canadiennes, et aussi de prendre part à des ateliers portant sur les difficultés de mettre sur pied un nouveau curriculum de premier cycle et sur les stratégies à employer ou à éviter. Bien que l'espace ne permette pas de faire état de toutes les discussions qui se sont déroulées, le recueil présente néanmoins chacune des allocutions prononcées dans le cadre de la conférence. Nous espérons que ces actes stimuleront dans les universités canadiennes les discussions portant sur le nouveau curriculum.

Nos remerciements vont aux membres du comité organisateur qui ont élaboré le programme de la rencontre à Ottawa: Mme Jane Gaskell, Mme Paule Leduc, M. Camille Limoges, M. Todd Smith, Mme Susan Trofimenkoff, M. Miles Wisenthal, M. Christian Pouyez et Mme Carol Bujeau.

Nous désirons également remercier le personnel de la Fédération : Mmes Sylvie Provost, Geneviève Régimbald et Carol Bujeau, qui ont pris tous les soins pour assurer la bonne marche de la conférence.

Nous exprimons aussi notre gratitude au Secrétariat d'État pour son généreux appui financier.

REMERCIEMENTS

De nombreux organismes et collègues nous ont été d'un précieux secours, tant dans l'élaboration du programme que par leur participation aux ateliers. Nous tenons à remercier particulièrement l'AUCC et l'ACPU d'avoir assuré une excellente couverture de la conférence dans leurs bulletins.

Nos remerciements s'adressent finalement à M. Christian Pouyez, ancien directeur général de la FCSS, qui a eu l'heureuse initiative d'organiser la conférence et dont le dévouement en a assuré le succès.

Gilles Paquet

LIBERAL EDUCATION
AS
SYNECDOCHE

> *May God us keep*
> *from single vision*
> *and Newton's sleep.*
> *William Blake*

1. INTRODUCTION

To the question WHO'S AFRAID OF LIBERAL EDUCATION?, the short answer is "a large number of people for a large number of good reasons" to paraphrase Professor Marriage, one of the conference speakers. We argue in this introductory chapter that the question is important not so much *per se*, but because of the light it throws on some fundamental issues in Canadian higher education.

What led the conference organizers to put forward this question was a wave of concern in Canada and the United States about the decay of cultural literacy, the suggestion that a change in postsecondary curricula might be the answer, and some recognition that the postsecondary enterprise was not doing much to put this solution in place. It was natural, under the circumstances, to inquire about the occult forces that might stand in the way of the implementation of this curative program; for there is some agreement on the seriousness of the originary concern about cultural literacy, even though there is no agreement about the sort of liberal education curriculum, if any, capable of dealing with this problem.

This introductory chapter, while emphasizing the importance of the debate on the liberal education curriculum, argues that there is a danger that the current crusade for a new classicism, if defined too narrowly, might lead well-intentioned higher education reformers in the

1

wrong direction, and allow the real challenges facing higher education to be occluded. There is undoubtedly a case for curriculum reform, but one that has to be approached from a broader and more global perspective than it has been by some defenders of the new classicism.

In section 2, a few signposts of the crisis facing the Canadian higher education enterprise are identified. In section 3, the challenge of crafting an education policy is characterized as a wicked problem : it is shown that goals are unknown or very ambiguous, and means-ends relationships very uncertain; institutional and epistemological traps facing educational reformers are identified. Section 4 sketches a way to conduct policy research in cases such as this. In conclusion, liberal education is shown to be part of a bigger problem, and it is suggested that it may be more fruitful to address the smaller issue in the context of the broader problem formulation.

This introduction goes somewhat beyond the questions raised by the main speakers and discussed in the workshops. As such, it may appear to be an oblique critique of the usual problematique underpinning the new classicism crusade. This is the case. The new classicism question deserves a different and more enlightening place in a richer and broader problematique. A subsidiary objective of this paper is to develop some interest in the launching of a policy research process likely to develop such a problematique.

2. A FEW SIGNPOSTS

a/Saskatoon

In October 1987, the National Forum on Post Secondary Education of Saskatoon in October 1987 staged true *états généraux* on higher education in Canada. One would have expected from these a comprehensive *cahier de doléances*. It did not materialize. A careful reading of the *Forum Papers*, the *Proceedings*, the workshops reports and the final recommendations reveals that the sensitivities of all parties in this first national chautauqua on higher education have stood in the way of fruitful discussion. In Saskatoon, debates were rendered aseptic by an excessive civility in the dialogue between lay persons and academics, and by the chronic Canadian obsession with federal-provincial sensitivities.

An unfortunate consequence has been the level of generality of the discussions and the weasel-nature of the consensus arrived at. It had been hoped that "l'esprit de Saskatoon" would guide educational reforms in Canada, but it was too feeble-hearted to do the job : it could not march on, it had to tiptoe all the time.

As a result, most of the contentious issues: the crisis of confidence in the higher education enterprise; the management of the postsecondary enterprise; the inadequacy of the curricula; and the need for a national strategy — all issues that had been well documented in the Proceedings of the Standing Senate Committee on National Finance (Leblanc 1987) — were carefully avoided. On the other hand, non-contentious issues, like promoting accessibility by marginal groups, and providing additional public financial resources to the postsecondary enterprise, became the foci of discussion.

The very generality of the discussions and recommendations allowed observers to use them as a Rorschach test, and to extract for special attention idiosyncratic themes — however fleetingly recurring. At the midpoint of the National Forum, Lise Bissonnette took advantage of her breakfast address to underline what she saw as "a renaissance of the concept of general education... a yearning for a new kind of classicism" (National Forum Proceedings 1987 : 81-82). This perception caught on. Given the fact that there was little of real substance on which the participants had developed a consensual view; Bloom's *The Closing of the American Mind* was a best-seller at the time (and so was Hirsch's *Cultural Literacy*), liberal education became a safe discussion item because it allowed everyone to address a truly academic issue, without the need for closer scrutiny of the performance of the higher education enterprise.

It is important to note that this "yearning" did not find a place in the concluding remarks of the Chairperson of the National Forum. Flexibility, adaptability, accessibility, federal-provincial cooperation, a better statistical data base, and a call for leadership were *les cris de ralliement* supposed to give a momentum to these *états généraux* and ensure that "l'esprit de Saskatoon" would live on. For obvious reasons, it did not.

b/le non-dit à Saskatoon et à Ottawa

The most surprising feature of the Saskatoon meeting was the implicit agreement of participants to exclude a variety of central institutional issues already well documented in an extensive literature on the crisis of the Canadian higher education enterprise : excessive provincialization; the rigidity and protected nature of higher education institutions; and the poverty of their management had been singled out repeatedly. Epistemological entrapments that stood in the way of reform were also ignored : the Rousseau-Dewey type of perception of education as content-free; the disciplinarization of knowledge production which triggered the emergence of methodism; a naive characterization of the way in which knowledge is acquired; the dominion of technical rationality, etc. (Emery 1980: Schon 1983; Neilson/Gaffield 1986; Hirsch 1987; Paquet/ von Zur Muehlen 1987; Watson 1987; Laplante 1988).

These issues might have been raised in the follow-up that many had anticipated for the National Forum, but that now seems unlikely. They were also excluded from the Ottawa conference, and this was especially true for the epistemological issues. Yet the epistemological questions are the truly revolutionary ones, because they are about fundamental aspects of knowledge acquisition, and can threaten more dramatically existing arrangements than mere institutional tinkering. It is understandable, therefore, that the vested interests of the postsecondary enterprise have ensured that they would not be raised in the open forum.

Liberal education is such an epistemological issue : it has to do with the sort of knowledge that needs to be acquired, given certain educational goals, *and* how it should be acquired. It represents a stratagem recommended by some educational reformers to accomplish objectives they regard as fundamental, yet the desirability of such a strategy can only be gauged by showing how it would make the postsecondary enterprise more effective as a system. This in turn requires that the whole process of education and education policy be clearly understood. This nexus of issues was hardly discussed.

c/entrapments highlighted

Lise Bissonnette's address in this volume indicates clearly that she is very pessimistic about the implementation of this "new classicism" curriculum for which there was supposedly such a "yearning" in Saskatoon. She ascribed this phenomenon to institutional obstacles standing in the way of the new curriculum (organizational sclerosis, pedagogical incapabilities, diversity of the clienteles, demands from the market place, and strong differences of opinion about the content of this new classicism).

In his comments on Lise Bissonnette's address, Howard Clark of Dalhousie University would appear to support her diagnosis: there is at present both a phenomenal pressure to promote specialization at the postsecondary level, *and* an equally phenomenal incapacity in the universities to do more than just cope. For Clark, the debate on curriculum is a symptom of the fundamental problems the postsecondary education institutions face.

Among other things, Mr. Grant's puzzling testimony in response to Bissonnette's paper urges postsecondary institutions to resist the private sector pressures to educate for utilitarian ends — but more importantly, he reveals the basic puzzlement of the business community when dealing with the higher education issue. As George Bernard Shaw diagnosed a long time ago, "every profession is a conspiracy against the laity," so it is hardly surprising that lay persons find it so difficult to come to terms with the crisis facing universities. In this case, both institutional and epistemological entrapments are ignored and simplistic suggestions ensue.

Dr. Karelis's analysis of the American scene helps to put things in perspective. The central question, he states, is "about the ends of general education and about the kind and type of general education that will best serve those ends."

Dr. Karelis refers to studies identifying many different purposes for education, all equally valid. From there, one may derive a wide range

4

of recipes to reach these different sets of objectives, yet none of these broad goals commands a core curriculum as a *sine qua non.* Indeed, the experiments at Harvard and Miami show a high degree of dissonance about these issues in the higher education system. Some have even argued that an enlightened education in a small number of typical concrete instances might —— John Dewey *dixit* —— provide an opportunity for a wide-ranging appreciation of historical, technological, social concerns, etc.

What is striking in Dr. Karelis's paper is evidence that the "public" and the "academy" appear to be at odds. Some parents in the United States want their children to be taught the traditional content or knowledge base they themselves were exposed to in their youth, while the academy would appear willing to supply only what its professoriate knows, that is, disciplinary knowledge. The romantically nostalgic public or the self-interested professoriate : who should decide what is needed?

d/experiments: a very small sample

Canadians have performed few experiments in search of a third way. As a result, the variety of available programs is much narrower in Canada than in the United States. A few of these experiments have been used to set the stage for discussion at the conference.

The first one sketches a strategy that is both timid and successful: the Arts One curriculum of the University of British Columbia - 60% of the first year student's specially designed and laid on. It has worked well for over twenty years for a very small cadre of students.

The second strategy is broader in scope : the liberal arts program proposed by the University of Toronto. This Unity of Knowledge program is intriguing; perhaps for that reason, it has not yet been implemented.

The third one summarizes a more ambitious strategy. It does not deal with liberal education directly; rather, it is an attempt to break down the monolithic structure of the university, and to create a quasi-market *within the university*; a separate entity —— *le module* —— (including professors, students and socio-economic agents) responsible for assessing the demand for courses making up programs, and another —— *la famille* —— (made up of the professoriate) responsible for supplying the courses. This is the system in place at the Université de Québec.

The first two strategies address the narrow question of what a liberal education curriculum might begin to look like; the third one is a strategy designed to shake loose the producer-dominated structure of universities, a factor held responsible by many observers of the postsecondary scene for the rigidities of university programs and their inadequacy.

As evidenced by the rich synthesis crafted by Michael Skolnik, the workshops' discussions roamed over a territory much wider than these few examples but, by and large, epistemological issues were not high on the agenda, and the range of institutional variables critically discussed remained relatively narrow.

This stems from two sets of implicit premises that remained largely unchallenged at the conference.

1/ A first unstated premise for many participants was the equation between cultural literacy as a needed currency, and liberal education as the only way to provide it. In fact, one may defend the importance of cultural literacy without any commitment to core curriculum or other paraphernalia of liberal education as a strategy (Hirsch 1987).

2/ Another major unstated premise for the participants at the conference was the presumed existence of a strong demand for liberal education. In fact, evidence for such a demand is difficult to gauge, and largely anecdotal. On the other hand, there is strong evidence of a growing demand for training and personal development activities, and massive sums of money have been spent on such activities by the public and private sectors. In Canada, we spend some $9 billion dollars for postsecondary education, through our universities and colleges, but at least another $3 billion is spent by business, trade associations, and public and private agencies to produce postsecondary education privately. Indeed, some have argued, on the basis of extensive interviews with firms and public agencies, that a much higher proportion of postsecondary education is produced by this shadow higher education system. To a certain extent, these activities are complementary to the postsecondary education publicly produced, but much of it is a substitute — a focused, practical, vocationally-oriented substitute for what the public regards as unsatisfactory output by postsecondary educational institutions (Paquet 1988b). This sort of massive investment would seem to raise questions about the view that postsecondary education should drift toward a new classicism.

3. EDUCATION POLICY : A WICKED PROBLEM

Education has always had a variety of functions in society : to produce literate responsible citizens; to acculture a heterogeneous citizenry; to develop the human capital necessary for the maintenance and improvement of economic growth, competitiveness and living standards; to allow individuals to develop character, self-awareness, interpersonal communication capabilities and competence; to develop mind and ability to reason (Peterfreund 1976). This is a complex task, and over time a variety of groups have crafted different strategies to realize diverse parts of this ambitious agenda.

Yet there is no indisputable notion of what the goals should be in a pluralistic society. Education policy poses an ill-structured problem to policy analysts, what Rittle and Webber have labeled a *wicked problem* (Rittel/Webber 1973). They note that ill-structured problems have two characteristics : (1) the goals are *not* known or are very ambiguous and (2) the means-ends relationships are highly uncertain and poorly understood. Rittel and Webber (1973) have spelled out some basic characteristics of wicked problems : they lack definitive formulation and a stopping rule as in a chess problem. In addition, solutions are not true-or-false but good-or-bad; every attempt at solving the problem counts significantly; and the planner has no right to be wrong.

a/ problématique

Educators, trainers and developers defend different approaches. For *educators*, operating in the Rousseau-Dewey tradition, the shaping of the mind and the ability to reason is somewhat content-neutral, and focused on general principles, on general knowledge; this is the way to learn how to think critically. For *trainers*, knowledge is skill and skill is knowledge, and there is no way to develop general transferable abilities without focusing on procedural and substantive schemata that are highly specific to the task at hand. For *developers*, the cornerstone might be loosely called an anthropological theory of education: knowledge and skills can be developed only on the basis of a capacity to grow as a human being within a human community to which one is accultured (Hirsch 1987).

These three notions are ideal-types in most discussions. In fact, much of what is done under any of these labels turns out to have educational, training and developmental components. Any curriculum, course or seminar may be represented as existing somewhere within a triangle of human capital formation, where each apex is an ideal-typical representation of each of these valuable types of human capital formation (Paquet 1988b).

FIGURE 1

The Human Capital Formation Triangle

personal
development

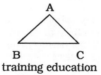

B   C
training education

The center of gravity of the traditional Canadian postsecondary enterprise (PSE) — and of any other national system for that matter — should be mappable as a point or as a zone within this triangle. It is

7

the resultant of a variety of private and public initiatives and policies that have privileged one component or another; moreover, all such systems have evolved through time, and their drift should be traceable within the triangle. Indeed, any PSE enterprise — ideally — should, through a diversity of institutions, cater to the diversity of private demands and public needs, for there are important differences in the strategies proposed by educators, trainers and developers : educators bet on C as the baseline, trainers on B, and developers on A.

In the 19th and early 20th centuries, the mix of education, training and development in traditional postsecondary education in Canada was probably more balanced than it is now. Much importance was given to each component of human capital formation, through a diversity of institutions and arrangements. During the first half of the 20th century, however, a formal philosophy of education, inspired by Jean-Jacques Rousseau and John Dewey came to be in good currency. It emphasized education as a formal process, shaping mind and reason that could be affected through content-neutral curricula. Education, as apex C, became the linchpin of the PSE. Segments of the PSE became more specialized, and a division of labour crystallized more sharply between the different institutions — universities, colleges, technical schools, etc. — some with a higher or a lower status depending on the mix of these components they provided. Personal development ceased to be a central variable in the PSE.

Technical schools, colleges and polytechnics developed a different brand of curriculum (more practical and more training-intensive) but the social status of these programs remained relatively low, and the training they purported to give became more and more "tainted" by the ruling educational philosophy. Within universities, training-intensive activities have also been given lower status and starved for resources. A recent report by the Canadian Chamber of Commerce was quite harsh in evaluating these institutions : the students are being trained on outdated equipment, and the quality of instruction is so low that "students graduate without sufficient skills or ability to pursue their chosen careers effectively" (Basken *et al.* 1988). Frank Stronach of Magna Corporation (in a personal interview) offered this very rationale for setting up his own training school.

b/ goals not known or ambiguous

This problematique does not suggest that postsecondary education should adopt a particular contour or should emphasize, as a matter of course, one of the three components. The education system must fit within the broader appreciative system that a society elects. Particular societies with quite different appreciative systems and norms may select quite different patterns of educational institutions located in different portions of the triangle of human capital formation. Identifying the underlying norms and specifying the required directions for curriculum reform are very difficult tasks,

8

for the basic goals are not agreed upon or even unambiguous in a pluralistic society.

For instance, the directions of curriculum policy will be quite different if post-secondary education is considered as *closed* (that is, independent of its social context) as opposed to being *open* (that is, seeing its survival as dependent on its capacity to adapt). In the same way, policy directions will be quite different if the post-secondary institution perceives its main goal as *training* individuals as opposed to *educating* them or to *developing* them into better human beings.

This leads to six quite different philosophies of postsecondary education, as can be seen in Figure 2, borrowed, in part, from Navarre/Paquet (Paquet/von Zur-Muehlen 1987 : Ch. VI).

FIGURE 2

Six philosophies of postsecondary institutions

depending on whether they are

		CLOSED SYSTEMS	OPEN SYSTEMS
with	TRAINING	science 1.1	technology 1.2
the main objective	EDUCATING	tradition 2.1	culture 2.2
of	DEVELOPING	perception 3.1	creativity 3.2

Position 1.1 corresponds to institutions wishing to train individuals in the scientific method as a universal value. Position 2.1 corresponds to institutions whose vocation is to train students to act in life in the light of a tradition used as an instrument to decode and make sense of the world. Position 3.1 corresponds to institutions that start from the individual and provide opportunities for fulfillment and self-improvement through improved perception. Position 1.2 corresponds to a vocation of training individuals in a way best suited to economic

development. In this case science is no longer sufficient; the institution must also take into account the technical needs of society, and the institution becomes a location for the development of highly skilled manpower. Position 2.2 corresponds to a situation where it is felt that a specialized and technical training does not suffice to ensure that individuals adapt well to an everchanging scene : the institution attempts then to be the locus for the production of culture in the sense of Clifford Geertz — a set of control mechanisms, of approaches and ways of defining problems, of "programs" in the sense that the computer scientist uses the term (Geertz 1965). Position 3.2 corresponds to institutions that emphasize creativity and the development of innovative power as a way to cope with a changing environment.

This is only a preliminary and somewhat simplistic stylization of possible goals and environmental conditions, but it illustrates how the general strategy of postsecondary institutions depends fundamentally on the definition of parameters such as those.

c/ institutional entrapments

The history of educational reforms is replete with failed attempts to direct the education system in different directions by means of institutional repairs. Traditional education practice has accommodated these innovations easily, particularly in times of affluence, when efficiency mattered little or when educational goals were over-ridden by other purposes: for example, keeping the baby-boomers off the street and out of the job market. When resources became scarce, the postsecondary education institutions felt threatened and reacted to pressure for change by making use of defense mechanisms to protect the existing ways. They evolved into a dynamically conservative system, that is to say, the system as a whole developed a tendency to remain the same and a capacity to resist change through a variety of means like unionization, etc.... (Paquet 1988a). At present, the postsecondary enterprise is not unlike the building industry — "a coalition of shared interests built on prevailing technologies" (Schon 1971).

For education is a social system and, as with all social systems, it contains a *structure*, a *technology*, and a *theory*. "The structure is a set of roles and relations among individual members. The theory consists of the views held within the social system about its purposes, its operations, its environment and its future. Both reflect, and in turn influence, the prevailing technology of the system" (Schon 1971). The best way to initiate change is to create a disequilibrium among these three components.

Changes in technology and in structure are easily neutralized by the existing institutions' "dynamic conservatism" viz. the numerous attempts to change the postsecondary enterprise by computerizing it or by imposing standardized curricula. The PSE has a capacity to repress such threats in much the same manner as bees in a beehive neutralize the danger when a mouse invades the beehive in winter. The bees sting the mouse to death, and then encapsulate it in wax; it looks alive, but it has become innocuous. The PSE finds it easy to prevent change by opposing or delaying it, or through continuous chanting that there is no existing problem in the postsecondary education enterprise that more public money could not cure. On the other hand, it finds it difficult to initiate real change because of the fact that the very technical and structural devices it might mobilize for change in its so-called collegial way are easily frustrated by internal systems (guilds, etc.) with their traditional conservatism.

It can be argued that it is quite different in the case of theory. Tampering with the way in which educationists perceive the world and themselves and the way in which they answer the question, what should we be doing? is very potent. It may appear more difficult to effect, but the likelihood of generating a truly creative disequilibrium and cumulative causation is much higher from that angle. While it is true that theorizing may be a tool for rationalizing away any alternative procedure as unsound, it is also a most powerful channel of attack when it can be shown that the whole knowledge production operation is wrongheaded.

d/ epistemology as lever

The positivist revolution, together with the Rousseau-Dewey tradition, shifted the center of gravity of the PSE by imposing a certain formalism in the postsecondary enterprise: there was more and more emphasis on theory, general principles and "methodism," and less and less on matters pertaining to the "oral," the "particular," the "local," and the "timely" (Paquet 1988a; Toulmin 1988). What has evolved in universities is a curriculum made up of a variety of general principles and broad surveys, providing the necessary elements for the educated person to learn to think critically. The idea of a true vocationally-oriented higher education system has disappeared [Gunderson 1978] and the ruling philosophy of education percolated down to the secondary level : even there, the skill component dwindled, and general content-free curricula prospered (Adams 1980).

But there has been a revival of practical philosophy in recent years, (Toulmin 1988) and the Rousseau-Dewey ruling philosophy of education has been challenged by recent work on cognition. Critical thinking, it would appear, evolves not from general content-free principles or methodologies, but from schemata that are highly specific to the task at hand and that are not easily transferable from one task to the next. Developing a human being is, therefore, ensuring that he or she acquires a fair number of such schemata, shared by others in the community, so as to be able to communicate competently and effectively with them — providing the person with a sort of "cultural currency" in the sense that economists give to existing national currencies (Hirsch 1987).

11

The development of this basic currency — capacious and vague, but fundamental to communicative competence and competitiveness — cannot be ensured either through general disembodied principles, in the manner of the traditional curricula, or simply through skill-building, in the manner one proceeds to coach an athlete to success. Facts and skills are inseparable and *background knowledge* —— even that which is specific culturally and nationally — is of great import in the development of critical reason, skills, and personal growth as a competent citizen. Traditionally, universities and colleges have provided through their core curriculum some smattering of background knowledge, but most often this has degenerated into formal general principles built into rigid curricula rather than being closely related to the national community, to the personal circumstances of students, and to schemata likely to be of use.

A revolution at the epistemological level is raising questions about existing structures and technologies in good currency in the PSE, and is therefore creating pressure for change. Indeed, it may be said that one of the reasons why the PSE has chosen to insulate itself from the teachings of its own schools of education or to belittle considerably the significance of what might be learned from them is that such insulation constitutes an apt defense mechanism.

From the work of Schon on the epistemology of practice flows a different image of educating, that is, of imparting knowledge. Schon shows that the dominant model of technical rationality wrongly presumes that knowledge flows from underlying disciplines (basic science) to applied science to actual performance of services to clients and society. For this narrow view of knowledge-flows — a sort of one-way street — he substitutes a two-way approach, emphasizing knowing-in-action/reflection-in-action, where knowledge emerges equally well from groping with situations and from surprises leading to on-the-spot experiments and knowledge-creation (Schon 1983).

The implications of this different approach to the professional education process are significant : an emphasis on the development of skills and a capacity for conversation with the situation though reflective practicum. It translates into a different curriculum (Schon 1987).

e/ how do we learn?

One should not presume that there is unanimity on the epistemological front. Research on cognitive skills is buzzing with competing paradigms and is characterized by strong disagreements among critics of the conventional wisdom at this point in time.

1/ Herbert Simon and others have been arguing that cognitive skills "depend on procedural and substantive schemata that are highly specific to the task at hand" and cast doubt (1) on the idea that there are any general or transferable cognitive skills and (2) on the Rousseau-Dewey tradition that has led us to believe that if students look at a few

12

cases, they will understand general principles and learn how to think critically (Hirsch 1987). This work maintains that much of education is the imparting of a large number of schemata, and that this requires "extensive knowledge of specifics."

In this system, the process of abstraction provides bridges from sensations to higher levels of thought. The ladder of abstraction goes from sensory data that provide repeated observations; from these, observed replicated associations emerge and are memorized; the knowledge gained by association is generalized by inference to classes of objects, and associations between classes of objects, such as those of cause and effect. Knowledge is thus the accumulation of these tried and true associations, and education becomes the distribution of accumulated knowledge (Emery 1980).

This approach departs from the Rousseau-Dewey tradition and re-introduces specifics (the local, the timely, the oral, the particular) into the process of knowledge acquisition. It does not go far enough, however, many observers would say, because of the fact that this approach remains based on a theory of perception that leaves much to be desired : "to perceive the world one must already have ideas about it. Knowledge of the world is explained by assuming that knowledge of the world exists. Whether the ideas are learned or innate makes no difference; the fallacy lies in circular reasoning" (Gibson 1979 : 304).

2/ An alternative paradigm starts from a different theory of perception, a theory of direct perception that has no need for a ladder of abstraction. This Gibsonian approach may be summarized as follows (Gibson 1979) :

1. the act of picking up information is a continuous act, an activity that is ceaseless and unbroken;
2. what is perceived are places, attached objects, detached objects, substances, together with events which are modifications of these things;
3. information is the specification of the observer's environment;
4. the perceptual system is a mode of overt attention: it can explore, investigate, adjust, optimize, extract;
5. the perceptual system registers persistence and change;
6. the process of information pick-up is susceptible to development and learning: better extracting, exploring, etc....

This new theory of active perception has important educational implications (Emery 1980) :

a/ since limitless information is available in the environment, access is restricted only by habits of perception;
b/ the perceptual systems can be improved : this is "an education in *searching* with our own perceptual systems, not an education in how to someday *research* in the cumulated pile of so-called social knowledge" (Emery 1980 : 29);
c/ education is "learning to learn" from our own perceptions.

This foray into cognitive psychology is not an aside : it is central to the main theme of education reform. For these shifts from general principles to schemata, and from schemata to direct perception, suggest different conceptions of knowledge, and consequently different notions of education. The further one moves away from a view of knowledge à la Rousseau-Dewey toward a view of knowledge à la Gibson (with the Simon-Hirsch view standing somewhat in the middle), the less persuasive is the case for a standard liberal education core curriculum.

In place of an educational system based on the accumulation of proven knowledge by memorization of established associations, rules of classification and logical inference, and built on the students' being taught to distrust their personal experience as a guide to knowledge (the goal is to produce a critical, disciplined and literate mind), one is led to suggest an educational system starting with the perception and experience of the individual, regarding education as the training of attention and higher studies as providing aided modes of apprehension or extraction of information (by means of instruments to allow metric knowledge; by means of language to make knowing explicit instead of tacit; and by means of pictures to extend perceiving and consolidate the gains of perceiving) (Gibson 1979; Emery 1980).

If one were to accept a Gibsonian view of the world, this means that knowledge is only restricted by our habits of perception, and that one may and must educate one's perceptual systems. This entails recentering education on the process of searching, on learning to explore and learn, for the weight of evidence is that even literate adults find it difficult to use their own perceptions.

This revolution in turn calls for an education process that puts much more emphasis on exploration and playfulness than is usually accepted in the postsecondary enterprise, for this is the way to enhance the capability to extract information from our worlds (March in March/Olsen 1976). The usual university insists above all that it must produce "disciplined intelligence... that is trained in logic and logical analysis" (Ross 1961). What is emerging from the new epistemology is a much broader approach that covers a variety of types of thinking — mathematical, logical, lateral, etc. (De Bono 1969) and this does not mesh well with the way in which the postsecondary enterprise perceives its vocation and its task (Paquet 1985).

4. EDUCATION REFORM AS SOCIAL LEARNING

At a time when the possibility of designing a liberal education curriculum is examined, it is essential to ascertain in some way what the ends of general education are and what kind or type of curriculum design is likely to lead in this direction in the light of what is known about cognition and learning.

On these questions, there is no clear *a priori* choice one can offer from the policy-maker's point of view among mixes of goals, or among theories of knowledge acquisition, or among institutional/-curricular arrangements likely to accomplish certain ends. This is the nature of a wicked problem. Policy analysts faced with ill-structured problems must *learn on the job* about both the configuration of facts and the configuration of values, but they must also manage to learn from the stakeholders in the policy game and from the many groups at the periphery who are in possession of important *local knowledge*, for without their participation no effective policy can be implemented.

Friedmann/Abonyi (1976) have stylized a *social learning model of policy research* to deal with these wicked problems : it combines a detailed analysis of four sub-processes : (1) the contruction of appropriate theories of reality depicting the *feasible*, (2) the formation of social values, that is, what is *acceptable*, (3) the gaming that leads to the design of political strategies in defence of the *stable* and the *implementable*, and (4) the carrying out of collective action ensuring *effectiveness* in implementation. These four interconnected sub-processes are components of a *social learning process* : any change in one affects the others (Friedmann 1979). This paradigm of social practice in policy research in depicted in a graph by Friedmann and Abonyi that is reproduced in Figure 3 below. In it, "cognition is linked to the world of events via social action and the result of that action. The adequacy of a theory of reality, and/or the political strategy is therefore dependent on the results of action and the extent to which these results satisfy the given social values" (Friedmann 1978).

Block B is the locus of dominant values that provide normative guidance either in the transformation of reality, or in the selection of strategies for action. Theory of reality (block A) refers to a symbolic representation and explanation of the environment; political strategy (block C) connotes the political game which generates the course of action chosen; social action (block D) deals with implementation and the interaction with periphery groups (Friedmann/-Abonyi 1976 : 88). Together these four sub-processes come to life in concrete situations.

Traditional approaches to policy research focus on attempts to falsify hypotheses about some objective reality according to the canons of scientific experimentation. This is too narrow a focus for policy research when the ground is in motion. For the *social practitioner*, what is central is an effort "to create a wholly new, unprecedented situation that, in its possibility for generating new knowledge, goes substantially beyond the initial hypothesis." The social learning paradigm is built on reflection-in-action, dialogue, mutual learning by experts and clients, that is, on an *interactive or transactive style of planning* : "the paradigm makes the important epistemological assumption that *action hypotheses* are verified as 'correct' knowledge only in the course of a social practice that includes the four components of theory (of reality), values, strategy and action. A further epistemological commitment is to the *creation of a new reality*, and hence to a new knowledge, rather than in

15

establishing the truth-value of propositions in abstraction from the social context to which they are applied" (Friedmann/Abonyi, 1976 : 838; Schon, 1983).

FIGURE 3

The Paradigm of Social Practice
in Policy Research

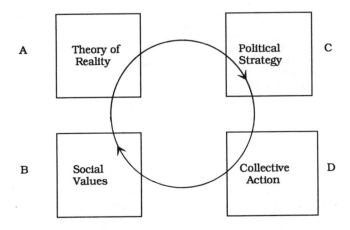

From FRIEDMANN AND ABONYI (1976) p. 88

5. CONCLUSION

The challenge put to the postsecondary enterprise by the epistemological revolution underway is bound to entail much more than the reshuffling of a few courses, or the development of a core curriculum, or the insertion in the curricula — one way or another — of the 5 000 essential names, phrases, dates and concepts to ensure "cultural literacy" — the Hirsch middle-of-the-road solution (Hirsch 1987). It forces a serious rethinking of what education is all about and it emphasizes the need to launch a social learning experiment to learn how "to learn how to learn."

The debate on liberal education has posed the problem of "the ends of general education and about the kind and type of general education that will best serve those ends" (Karelis). In that sense, it has put on the front burner an issue that the postsecondary enterprise has been refusing to face for some time now.

Those arguing for liberal education must establish why such a strategy would effect better whatever postsecondary education wants to do; and we are back to the more general questions raised above. These more general questions have to be probed if one is to be able to put forward a strategy likely to be effective. Yet, there is no way learn about these issues except through action hypotheses.

The challenge put forward by the liberal education debate cannot therefore be resolved *a priori*. It cannot be resolved in isolation either. What is required is a broadly based social inquiry into the problems of higher education very much on the model of the Energy Options process launched in 1987 to provide an opportunity for a dialogue among Canadians about the common energy future. The report in 1988 (Kierans 1988) showed that much had been learned within one year through a process of wide consultation with all interested parties and groups throughout the country. It may well be that nothing less than such a process can bring about a clarification of the objectives of our education system and an answer to the questions about the kind and type of postsecondary education we should design for our grandchildren. The process is difficult to manage and does not always generate unambiguous or satisfactory answers (Paquet 1988c); moreover it is not likely that such a broad consultation can be engineered easily given the federal-provincial quagmire surrounding all issues educational in Canada. But such an inquiry may be the only vehicle likely to generate the sort of debate on postsecondary education that is so urgently needed. Higher education is not a problem any easier to tackle than biculturalism of transportation, so there is no reason that anything short or an inquiry of the sort suggested is likely to bring forth the feasible, acceptable and implementable solutions we are looking for.

Some may argue that we have shifted the debate from a simple question about liberal education to the broad question of higher education in general. This is undoubtedly true. One of the characteristics of wicked problems is that they often are a symptom of a "higher order problem." Thus crime in the street may simply be a symptom of general moral decay, lack of opportunity, poverty etc. (Rittel/Webber 1973). In the same manner, the liberal education debate is an echo of a higher order malaise in the postsecondary education system. It may also be true that the malaise in education simply reflects some still higher order malaise in our society. The best way to deal with lower order issues is not to deal with them in a restrictive way if they are only symptoms. One might be more effective by tackling the problem on as high a level as possible.

ADAMS, R.J. (1980) "Training in Canadian Industry : Research, Theory and Policy Implications" Hamilton : McMaster University/Faculty of Business/Research & Working Papers Series No. 168, April.

BASKEN, R. *et al* (1988) *Focus 2000 - Report of the Task Force on Harnessing Change*, Ottawa/Montreal/Toronto; The Canadian Chamber of Commerce.

BLOOM, A. (1987) *The Closing of the American Mind*, New York : Simon & Schuster.

DE BONO, E. (1969) *The Mechanism of Mind*, Harmondsworth : Penguin.

EMERY, F. (1980) *Educational Paradigms - An Epistemological Revolution* (mimeo) December.

FRIEDMANN, J. (1978) "The Epistemology of Practice : A Critique of Objective Knowledge" *Theory and Society*, 6, 1, July.

FRIEDMANN, J. (1979) *The Good Society*, Cambridge, Mass. : The MIT Press.

FRIEDMANN, J./ ABONYI, G. (1976) "Social Learning : A Model for Policy Research" *Environment and Planning*, A., Vol. 8.

GEERTZ, C. (1965) "The Impact of the Concept of Culture on the Concept of Man" in J.R. Platt (ed.) *New Views of Man*, Chicago : The University of Chicago Press.

GIBSON, J.J. (1979) *The Ecological Approach to Visual Perception*, Boston : Houghton Mifflin.

GUNDERSON, M. (1978) "Training in Canada : Progress and Problems" in B.O. Pettman (ed.) *Government Involvement in Training*, Bradford : MCB Publications.

HIRSCH, E.D. Jr (1987) *Cultural Literacy*, Boston : Houghton Mifflin.

KIERANS, T. *et al* (1988) *Energy and Canadians into the 21st Century*, Ottawa : Energy, Mines & Resources.

LAPLANTE, L. (1988) *L'université - questions et défis*, Québec : Institut québécois de recherche sur la culture.

LEBLANC, F.E. (1987) *Federal Policy on Post-secondary Education*, Report of the Standing Senate Committee on National Finance (under the Chairmanship of F.E. Leblanc), Ottawa : Supply & Services.

MARCH, J.C. (1976) "The Technology of Foolishness" in J.G. March/J.P. Olsen (eds.) *Ambiguity and Choice in Organizations*, Oslo : Universitetsforlaget.

NATIONAL FORUM ON POST-SECONDARY EDUCATION (1987) *Proceedings*, Halifax, N.S. : The Institute for Research on Public Policy.

NATIONAL FORUM ON POST-SECONDARY EDUCATION (1987) *The Forum Papers*, Halifax, N.S. : The Institute for Research on Public Policy.

NEILSON, W.A.W./ GAFFIELD, C. (1986) *Universities in Crisis : A Mediaeval Institution in the Twenty-first Century*, Montreal : The Institute for Research on Public Policy.

PAQUET,G. (1985) "Entrepreneurship et Université : le combat de Carnaval et Carême" Revue de gestion des petites et moyennes organisations.

PAQUET, G. (1988a) "Two Tramps in Mud Time or The Social Sciences and Humanities in Modern Society" in B. Abu-Laban/ B.G. Rule (eds.) *The Human Sciences*, Edmonton : The University of Alberta Press.

PAQUET, G. (1988b) "Training and Development : The Shadow Higher Education System in Canada" R.A. Watts [ed.] *Canada/United Kingdom Colloquium on Post-secondary Education*, London : Gower Press (in press).

PAQUET, G. (1988c) "A Social Learning Framework for a Wicked Problem : The Case of Energy" (mimeo 24p.).

PAQUET, G./von Zur Muehlen, M. (1987) *Education Canada? Higher Education on the Brink*, Ottawa : The Canadian Higher Education Research Network.

PETERFREUND, S. (1976) "Education in Industry - Today and in the Future" *Training and Development Journal*, 30, 5, May.

RITTEL, H.W./ WEBBER, M.M. (1973) "Dilemmas in a General Theory of Planning" *Policy Sciences*, 4.

ROSS, M.G. (1961) *The New University*, Toronto : University of Toronto Press.

SCHON, D.A. (1971) *Beyond the Stable State*, New York : Random House.

SCHON, D.A. (1983) *The Reflective Practioner*, New York : Basic Books.

SCHON, D.A. (1987) *Educating the Reflective Practioner*, San Francisco : Jossey-Bass Publishers.

TOULMIN, S. (1988) "The Recovery of Practical Philosophy" *The American Scholar*, 57, 3.

WATSON, C. (1987) *Governments and Higher Education - The Legitimacy of Intervention*, Toronto : The Ontario Institute for Studies in Education.

Lise Bissonnette

LA FORMATION FONDAMENTALE : AU DELÀ DES CLICHÉS

Il est de mise de remercier, avant toute chose, les gens qui vous invitent à prononcer l'allocution d'ouverture d'une conférence aussi imposante. Entre nous, je ne suis pas sûre, en cet instant même, de ne pas en vouloir un peu à Caroline Andrew, qui a tant insisté pour que je me mette au blanc sur la question de la formation fondamentale, c'est-à-dire, au fond, sur la nécessité de la vertu. Je la remercie, donc, mais avec des réserves. Si je connaissais quelque chose au contenu de la vertu, à sa pratique, je serais sans doute entrée au cloître, comme l'a fait ma soeur aînée. Il est donc hors de question que je tente de vous en tracer le programme. Pour me sortir de ce discours, toutefois, je peux vous parler quelque temps des énormes difficultés qu'il y a à la pratiquer.

Let us start by clearing up some misunderstandings. My own involvement with the present debate on the return to liberal education goes back to the National Conference on Post-Secondary Education, held last fall in Saskatoon. I did not participate very actively in the discussions; I was hired as a listener, an intelligent one, the organizers hoped, with the task of summarizing the workshops' discussions. I worked during the night, trying to make something out of 21 handwritten reports coming from as many groups, each of which had been designed by computer to represent every Canadian constituency you can think of, from a school board commissioner in Yukon, to a French-speaking business student from the Maritimes, including a college

21

principal from rural Ontario. The synthesis of such a crisscrossing of different minds and experiences should have resulted in an awful patchwork. I was astounded to discover that it had not. I might have been suffering from a case of late-night fogged vision, but I detected an extraordinary degree of consensus in what I was reading, and trying to make sense out of.

The message, from all these people, was that they wanted schools, colleges, and universities less obsessed with technical, professional, specialized training, and more devoted to giving students the fundamentals of quality general education. Knowingly or not, given the state of our generation's own general culture, they were rediscovering the old saying from Montaigne : *Mieux vaut une tête bien faite qu'une tête bien pleine.* I was struck, however, not so much by the enthusiasm of the participants for such a proposal, as by a kind of nostalgia. They seemed to think that something had been lost along the path of modern education that used to be there before. Their quest seemed to be for a "new classicism," the kind of general education one used to get in our typical "collèges classiques" in Québec before the Quiet Revolution, or in the elite Liberal Arts colleges where some can still afford to go in the United States or Ontario.

The idea was that if you could add some modern ingredients into the former ideal curriculum, let us say if you could marry computer literacy with philosophy, or a knowledge of basic modern genetics with history, and then if you could make all of the results available to all post-secondary students across Canada, we would finally put education back on the right track. There was otherwise total dissatisfaction with the system as it is. When I summarized my findings, on the day after, I think I made some caveats that were not heard. The term "a new classicism" was however an instant success, and it found a triumphant way in the synthesis document which the federal government saw fit to publish with some fanfare a few months later. Mind you, being a strong opponent to federal involvement in higher education, I was a little distressed at being used as the flagship of a new era. Federal literature, however, is not widely read and discussed in Québec, and I got away with the whole misunderstanding until Caroline came to me.

Now, at last, you know why I am going to skirt around the issue, and why I have no intention of telling you what should be included in this "new classicism," and why I am going to concentrate instead on the endless difficulties I foresee for those of you who dream of getting there.

Let us deal first with the reasons why such a remarkable consensus has built around the necessity of a return to liberal education, over the last decade. The sixties and the seventies, as all of us know who went through the education system during that period, were a time when the idea of specialized education blossomed. Former Canadian elites were made of generalists, brilliant ones very often, but the job market, the technological and technocratic revolution was calling for minds of a different kind, deeply knowledgeable about special issues and techniques. Barely in their pre-teen years, kids had to be earmarked according to their literary or scientific aptitudes, and then pushed where they seemed to do best. High schools became experts at streaming, categorizing, mapping avenues for the future specialists and, of course, they dumped the others along the way. Colleges and universities did the same with more sophistication and good conscience.

Faced with the results, there are a few things we all agree not to like and about which everybody is complaining :

- though they are still expecting colleges and universities to churn out the best specialists with perfect knowledge of their wares, employers are unhappy with graduates who are not flexible enough to adjust to a changing environment, or to assume larger assignments. Some in the United States, I am told, (would you believe it!) are even hiring social scientists to act as an antidote to the narrow technical thinking their enterprise is now struggling with.
- you and I, and parents generally, and publishers especially, are complaining wildly about graduate illiteracy : a perception that these young people don't know how to read, let alone write properly, and that some can only count with the help of a pocket calculator, if at all.
- another cause for wide discontent is the next generation's moral sense. While not being exactly saints ourselves, we have a tendency to think that they are often even worse, that they have lost the basic capacity to discriminate between good or bad. The Ivan Boesky case, an American scandal of major proportions over insider trading, led many to question the ethics of the whole yuppie generation. Ethics professors got their jobs back, and some even got hired. We all feel, however, that ethics should be part of the basic curriculum, instead of being administered as a last minute vaccine, before young people are launched in the great race to make money.
- more generally, we are beginning to realize that we really outdid ourselves when it came to history. Not only do you get a blank stare when talking about anybody of some notoriety or fame who lived between the days of Adam and Eve and of Maurice Duplessis, but you realize, with some nightmarish fear, that the Second World War and its crucial lessons for civilization might have no more meaning, for the coming generations, than a made-for-TV docudrama.

You can certainly add your own findings to this short list but the basic feeling, largely shared on this continent and in Europe, is that our latest educational models might have contributed to the advancement of knowledge but, at the same time, they have also shrunken the minds of mankind. It is about time, of course, that we do something about it.

Il n'y a pas de véritable consensus s'il n'apparaît quelqu'un, quelque part, qui dise magnifiquement ce que tout le monde pense sans trop pouvoir l'articuler. C'est dans ce contexte qu'apparaît le maître à penser de la formation fondamentale, la star actuelle du monde de l'éducation, le professeur Allan Bloom, l'auteur du best seller *The Closing of the American Mind* (en français *L'Âme désarmée*).

Remarquez que M. Bloom existait depuis longtemps, et qu'il répétait toujours la même chose, y compris quand il enseignait à Toronto il y a vingt ans. Il nous rappelle lui-même, dans cet ouvrage touffu, comment on se moqua de lui sur les campus américains des années soixante. Autrement dit, ce n'est pas faute de prophètes que nous nous sommes trompés, mais c'est là une autre histoire.

Le triomphe de M. Bloom, et son art, c'est d'avoir résumé (longuement et en allant jusqu'à régler ses comptes avec les philosophes allemands) notre malaise. Au nom de nos nouvelles valeurs, comme la quête d'égalité sociale, l'anti-racisme, le féminisme, le tiers-mondisme, le pacifisme, dit-il, nous avons jeté par-dessus bord les qualités en même temps que les défauts de nos anciennes valeurs. La quête de la vérité, de la clarté, de la vertu, de la passion, de la beauté a cédé la place à une idéologie égalisatrice où nul ne trouve plus de points de repères. On dit : toutes les civilisations sont égales et nous n'avons pas à poser de jugement même sur les plus barbares, mon idée vaut celle de mon voisin et celle d'Aristote en passant, toutes les différences sont culturelles entre l'homme et la femme comme entre l'Orient et l'Occident et nul point de vue, nulle part, n'a de titre à l'emporter sur un autre. Bloom, évidemment, dénonce violemment cet état de confusion intellectuelle et mentale et réaffirme que, si la société ne veut pas aller jusqu'à perdre le sens du bien et du mal, il lui faut admettre à nouveau qu'il y a des vérités, qu'il y a une hiérarchie des valeurs, et qu'une religion qui interdit le meurtre rituel vaut mieux qu'une autre où il est permis, que l'histoire n'est pas entièrement fausse parce qu'elle a été écrite en ignorant l'existence des femmes ou des noirs, et que Michael Jackson n'est pas l'égal de Mozart.

En France, au même moment, et par la plus parfaite des coïncidences, semble-t-il, le philosophe et écrivain bien connu Alain Finkielkraut publiait *La Défaite de la pensée*, une attaque en règle contre le relativisme culturel dont souffre notre époque, et l'éducation française autant que l'éducation américaine. Comme Bloom qui réclame le retour aux "grands livres" (Great Books) de notre civilisation, Finkielkraut renvoyait au siècle des Lumières. L'Occident, disait-il, n'a pas à s'excuser d'avoir généré le concept de démocratie, d'avoir vénéré la liberté, d'avoir fait progresser la science et, à travers tout cela, l'humanité. Il faut donc redonner aux jeunes la mémoire des valeurs qui se sont transmises jusqu'à eux, et la conviction qu'il existe de grandes vérités, de vrais repères, que l'honnête homme (et femme, comme ajoute tout de même aujourd'hui) doit connaître et embrasser.

Les critiques de ces livres magistraux, venant à la bonne heure, ont porté comme vous le savez sur leur caractère nostalgique et élitiste. À lire Bloom, on a l'impression que toutes les universités doivent être réorganisées autour du département de philosophie, où les ressources doivent se concentrer autour des meilleurs esprits. Solution un peu courte dans un monde où tous les campus ne sont pas de bucoliques Yale ou de charmants Harvard, et où des dizaines de milliers d'étudiants s'entassent dans les labyrinthes des universités urbaines pour acquérir les diplômes spécialisés que des millions d'employeurs ne sont pas à la veille de cesser de requérir.

Ce dont nous rêvons, quand nous parlons de formation fondamentale dans des colloques comme celui de Saskatoon et sans doute comme celui-ci, c'est plutôt de trouver des moyens de donner au plus grand nombre les repères essentiels de la culture. Nous aimons l'analyse de Bloom mais, pour ceux qui oeuvrent dans le domaine de l'éducation, elle laisse le problème entier. C'est pourquoi j'ai une estime toute particulière pour un autre philosophe, bien québécois celui-là, qui a décidé de s'attaquer pratiquement au problème. Jacques Dufresne, que plusieurs d'entre vous connaissent sûrement, a entrepris rien moins que de rédiger un ouvrage monumental, qui s'appellera *Les Routes du savoir*, où il cherche à retracer une cinquantaine de pistes des connaissances que devrait posséder une tête contemporaine bien faite. Faire la synthèse éthique, philosophique, historique, scientifique qui convient à notre époque, c'est encore possible, selon lui. Nous attendrons le résultat avec impatience, je ne connais pas d'entreprise semblable.

Même si elle réussissait, toutefois, elle laisserait entier le problème des éducateurs qui oeuvrent sur le terrain, et qui veulent redessiner le curriculum des collèges et des universités pour qu'il convienne à ces nouveaux objectifs et qu'il soit accessible au plus grand nombre. Je suppose, en effet, que nul d'entre nous n'est prêt à remettre en cause l'acquis extraordinaire, et en bien des cas inachevé, qu'est la démocratisation de l'enseignement supérieur au Canada.

Pourtant, si notre idéal de ramener à l'école un "nouveau classicisme" est plus qu'un slogan dont on continuera pendant quelque temps à se gargariser dans les colloques, il faudra bien s'atteler à des réformes concrètes. Quand j'ai entrepris d'en dresser la liste, je me suis fait peur à moi-même. Mais comme j'ai démissionné de l'enseignement dès ma première tentative, et que vous ne l'avez pas fait, j'imagine que nous ne sommes pas de la même trempe et je vous livre ma liste en toute confiance. Elle a au moins un avantage : si vous la transformiez en projets à soumettre au Conseil de recherches en sciences humaines du Canada, vous auriez de quoi créer tout ce qu'il faut d'emplois en sciences sociales pour occuper toutes les personnes-années que vous formez actuellement, et qui n'ont pas terriblement d'avenir dans le virage technologique.

Voici donc, dans l'ordre croissant de difficulté, comment je vois la course à obstacles dans laquelle on s'engage quand on parle de formation fondamentale autrement que pour le plaisir, et la bonne conscience, d'en parler.

I am going to give you a list of the obstacles you are facing if you are serious about your overall objectives. I have organized them in five categories, and you could obviously add some more :

LISE BISSONNETTE

1. ORGANIZATIONAL PROBLEMS

Let us suppose for a minute that you want to create a basic curriculum with all the ingredients that should be included in a modern general education. Let us say that you (the principal, the professors, the student council and all other institutional bodies you have to negotiate with in this day and age) have even agreed on the content of such an ideal common curriculum for all college or undergraduate students (we shall come back to the content problem later).

The whole system, as it has been built and computer built-in over the last twenty years, will be, as you know, against you. I am thinking here of schedules and classroom space, which are in turn determined by registration processes and the cafeteria-type curriculum, the only one these students have ever learned to cope with and to get credits for. Professor workloads are cut to fit with this model, as are the collective agreements governing these workloads. It is an atomized but comfortably measurable universe, where three credits for a philosophy course equal three credits for one in photography or sometimes in martial arts.

If you want to make sense out of this and if you want to put in place a real core program where students will get the basics of a general culture, you obviously will have to go further than putting together a package of required courses in philosophy, literature, mathematics, French or English, history and, in the new fad, a basic course in the technological civilization. These packages already exist in CEGEPs and colleges and what you end up with is still an atomized education the students cannot make sense out of.

I am not saying that this cannot be done today. You all know about experiments along these lines. But if we are serious about correcting the whole system, about making such a desirable arrangement available to the whole student population, we are literally talking about dismantling the organizational process as it now stands in our institutions. We are talking about dismantling the most sophisticated bureaucratic and technocratic arrangements in the history of education. I wish you good luck.

2. PEDAGOGICAL PROBLEMS

This is a topic very dear to my heart. When I hear or read discussions about the need for a better general or liberal education, I am struck by the amount of magic thinking involved. It is as though, once you had agreed on what should be taught, anybody with a license for teaching in any institution would suddenly be able to be part of this immense task. We forget the obvious: most of the professors who now teach in our colleges and universities have been hired according to only one criterion, their specialized training. To this day, when you read the career ads in newspapers, the listed requirements for college or university

26

postings never mention either pedagogical training or a tested ability to teach. Since the sixties, pedagogy, above the high school level, has been the last thing on our minds.

And yet there we are, dreaming of a reform where our students should be taught by the likes of Socrates, mentors and guides for their minds, able to reach out of their subject matters to the realities of the large world. Time and again, we have been told, and forcefully by students, that teaching should be reinstated as a prestigious function in our institutions, instead of being considered as a fourth-class job after research, publication, and program managing. I see no sign, anywhere, of good professors being praised, valued, honoured for what they are as pedagogues. And as long as I don't see those signs, I simply will not believe that the present rhetoric about the return to general education is sincere, and that it is anything more than an intellectual fad.

3. PROBLEMS OF CLIENTELE

Whom do we want to be the recipients of this blessed gift of a good general education? I gather that we are not talking about the very few who can afford it, whether by birth or scholastic achievement. What I hear and read about seems to be a curriculum reform for all of those who crowd our colleges and universities. They are not, however, as homogeneous as they used to be. Their ages vary widely, from teenagers to adult learners sitting in the same classroom. Their social and economical backgrounds are also very diverse. Half of our university student population, in Québec, is registered on a part-time basis and a large portion, especially in some regional universities where they often are the majority, are engaged in short-term programs, supposedly made to order for the job market, and I see such a trend growing elsewhere in Canada (these programs are great moneymakers for universities).

The pattern I see coming is one where full-time students will benefit from whatever curriculum reform we will be able to manage to give them and they will benefit from a better basic education. Full-time students, as you know, also tend to be the more well-to-do, the sons and daughters of the middle classes and up, and of the traditional intellectual elites. Others will have to be satisfied with the kind of patchwork education we are now delivering without regard for the end product. The two-speed university is already a reality, where a sort of "ivy league core" coexists with the masses, and where these undistinguished masses indirectly subsidize the best and most expensive programs you can only engage in if you can afford a full-time education. I have no doubt that medical, science, and engineering faculties will be the first to engage successfully in curriculum reform, and to find the resources to make it work. Once they succeed, and once their graduates get out into the larger world with a larger view of the same world, the alarm for a better core curriculum will disappear.

4. PROBLEMS OF OUTPUT

I have heard a lot of business people, Board of Trade and Chambre de Commerce representatives, participants in provincial and federal economic summits join the chorus claiming for a return to a kind of liberal arts education where basics are basics, where students "learn to learn" as the cliché goes, instead of cramming knowledge into an otherwise confused mind. To tell you the truth, I simply cannot stomach these sugary pronouncements. We live in a society more obsessed than ever by the high-technology race, and the job market is still basically hoping that high schools, colleges, and universities will produce highly skilled technicians in droves. From time to time there is a need for someone with a more open mind and some ability for interpersonal relations, or a need for someone with some political understanding to negotiate with a union, or to negotiate with a government of the work environment to get a subsidy. From time to time, you also need senior executives who can devise a long-term strategy taking into account the political climate for investment in Third World countries, or who can go to a fundraising dinner for an artistic company without sounding too philistine. That is when you get a bit angry with business or engineering schools as they are, and when you ask for a bit more of a general education in the graduate you hire. Generally, however, you do not mind if the general workforce knows little about history, about our political and constitutional ways and institutions, and about Leibniz's crucial influence on the civilization of the computer.

Despite the euphoria of the Saskatoon conference, and the great federal enthusiasm for the concept of a "new classicism," what you see is what you get. Ottawa is cutting down on the general transfer payments to the provinces earmarked for general education purposes, and putting the money back into education programs, yes, but programs which fit its own view of what education should be. There, you do not hear about "general" or "liberal" or "fundamental" education, or "new classicism" anymore. You hear about manpower training, period. That is the real world, and governments simply respond to the pressure of the real world.

5. LES VALEURS

J'ai gardé l'obstacle le plus énorme pour la fin, comme il se doit. Il s'agit de la question des valeurs.

Supposons un instant que nous aurions réglé tout le reste, réformé nos modes d'organisation, formé ou trouvé de vrais pédagogues, démocratisé l'accès à l'excellence et non seulement à nos bâtiments scolaires, et convaincu les employeurs de ce monde qu'ils gagneront plus à engager des têtes mieux faites que des têtes plus pleines de virages technologiques. Il nous reste à nous entendre sur ce que contiendrait une formation fondamentale, alliant à la fois la mémoire de l'humanité dont nous sommes et l'appartenance à l'époque où nous vivons.

L'Université Stanford, qui n'est pas la plus bête, s'y est essayée récemment et elle en brûle encore. En cette rentrée de 1988, elle met en vigueur un nouveau programme de cours obligatoires de premier cycle où on a laissé tomber quelques classiques de la littérature occidentale pour les remplacer par l'enseignement d'ouvrages par des "femmes, des minorités, et des personnes de couleurs", qu'on dirait ici des "minorités visibles". Le curriculum comprendrait désormais des extraits de l'Ancien et du Nouveau Testament, des oeuvres de Platon, saint Augustin, Machiavel, Rousseau, Marx, ainsi que de nouveaux classiques avec au moins un accent sur une "culture non européenne". En les enseignant, il faudra porter une attention particulière, dit le programme, "aux problèmes de race, de genre et de classes sociales".

De quoi faire rugir Allan Bloom et tous ses nouveaux disciples instantanés, qui considèrent qu'une grande oeuvre est une grande oeuvre, qu'elle ait été écrite par un mâle blanc ou par une femme noire, et qu'on est encore en train de tordre des vérités historiques en prétendant, au contraire, redresser l'histoire. D'autres diront, au contraire, qu'il n'y a là que justice parce que les grands livres ont été jugés tels par des civilisations antérieures qui faisaient fi de tout ce qui n'était pas la pensée occidentale masculine, et que les étudiants devraient être initiés autant à Confucius et à Mahomet qu'à saint Augustin en cette période où nous faisons irruption en Asie et où l'Asie fait irruption chez nous.

Bref, la querelle est ouverte. Il est vraisemblable et sans doute souhaitable que les réformistes la gagnent. Personnellement, je trouve scandaleux de voir par exemple s'instaurer des compétitions scolaires au sein de la francophonie (comme l'émission Génies en herbe) où l'on attend de jeunes Africains qu'ils identifient la musique de Gilles Vigneault ou le nom du président de la quatrième république française, et où en contrepartie les jeunes Québécois et Français ne se font jamais embêter sur la géographie et l'histoire africaine, à part, peut-être, de devoir identifier Léopold Senghor. C'est dire que nos curriculums sont à l'avenant, et que la culture générale de notre époque non seulement est rarement enseignée, mais qu'elle n'est pas du tout repensée. Quand nous nous y mettrons, toutefois, nous devons savoir que c'est le genre de controverse que connaît Stanford qui nous attend.

Rattaché à ce problème de contenu est celui du débordement des connaissances. Il serait évidemment plus facile d'additionner les grands auteurs que de choisir, mais il faut choisir, ce qui nous ramène constamment à nos valeurs. En avons-nous, ou les avons-nous sacrifiées au nom du relativisme culturel, comme dit Bloom? Si oui, lesquelles voulons-nous affirmer? Dirons-nous, comme Alain Finkielkrant, qu'il faut cesser d'avoir honte d'être des Occidentaux et se restituer fièrement dans la civilisation qui fut le berceau du progrès, de la science, de la démocratie? Ou accepterons-nous, comme nous le demande l'Orient, de reconnaître la plénitude et l'égalité d'une autre civilisation?

Quels sont, enfin, les grands noms du temps présent? Le nouveau classicisme ne doit pas simplement élargir les références du passé, asseoir Rosa Luxembourg à côté de Karl Marx, ou ranger le Coran à côté de la Bible. Il doit proposer des esprits qui font la synthèse de cette fin de siècle, qui lisent et interprètent notre environnement, nos conflits, la planète comme nous l'avons transformée. Voilà la question à laquelle Allan Bloom ne répond pas. Nous avons passé les valeurs anciennes par dessus bord sans les remplacer, dit-il avec quelque raison. Mais on ne peut non plus y retourner par défaut. Il faut retrouver de la mémoire, sans aucun doute, mais aussi une intelligence du présent, et si possible de l'avenir. Il doit bien y avoir, encore, des auteurs de grands livres.

Ces choix ne se retrouveront pas dans un nouveau curriculum en brassant les ingrédients comme dans une recette de cuisine. Ils sont les plus difficiles qu'on puisse faire, et ils sont peut-être impossibles dans des sociétés où l'homogénéité, sans parler de l'unanimité, n'existe tout simplement plus.

Je n'affirme pas, toutefois, que la liste des obstacles que je viens de présenter est un bloc absolument insurmontable et qu'il faut baisser les bras. J'en ai cependant assez, vous l'aurez compris, des discours sur le sujet. Quand j'ai suivi mon premier cours de pédagogie, il y a de cela plus de vingt ans, l'admonestation de Montaigne sur les têtes bien faites à préférer aux têtes bien pleines était déjà un disque usé. Je n'ai jamais entendu rien d'autre, de l'École normale à la Faculté des sciences de l'Éducation, dans les montagnes de littérature pédagogique que j'ai lues par la suite, de Célestin Freinet au rapport Parent, du frère Untel à Allan Bloom, qu'une vaste exhortation à préparer des jeunes êtres à "apprendre à apprendre", à avoir une large vision du monde, à éduquer le jugement et l'esprit en même temps qu'à communiquer des connaissances. L'humanisme, la prétention de former plutôt que de simplement informer, se retrouvent dans toute la rhétorique de toutes nos institutions depuis qu'on a appris à rédiger des discours sur les objectifs, à former des comités pour s'auto-étudier et à faire des colloques pour y réagir. Il n'y a rien, mais rien de nouveau sous le soleil.

Je croirai que cette préoccupation est vraie, qu'elle n'est pas une mode, quand je la verrai devenir une obsession sur le terrain d'une école, d'un collège, d'une université. J'y croirai quand je verrai le souffle atteindre les établissements publics, la clientèle adulte, les étudiants à temps partiel. J'y croirai quand je verrai les conventions collectives rétrécir, les procédures administratives se réduire, et grandir proportionnellement la réflexion sur le curriculum. J'y croirai quand les bibliothèques seront plus urgentes à bâtir que les centres informatiques ou les centres sportifs. J'y croirai surtout, petit

détail qui m'est clair, quand les universités décerneront leurs docto-
rats honoris causa tout autant à leurs meilleurs pédagogues qu'aux indi-
vidus qui les financent et aux seuls diplômés qui ont fait des décou-
vertes scientifiques de pointe. J'y croirai enfin quand il faudra
savoir enseigner pour devenir enseignant. Si jamais cela arrivait, le
débat sur les valeurs, sur le contenu à inscrire au curriculum serait
peut-être vif, interminable, ouvert à perpétuité. On s'interrogerait
toujours sur ce qui doit être fondamental, dans la formation fondamentale. Mais le mot formation, enfin, aurait peut-être un sens.

Jon K. Grant

THOUGHTS
ON
THE THREE SOLITUDES —
BUSINESS, GOVERNMENT
AND THE UNIVERSITIES

Thank you very much for inviting me to address the Social Science Federation of Canada's Conference "Who's Afraid of Liberal Education". As a token businessman at your conference I am not all that sure what you expect of me. For the past fifteen years, I have found myself increasingly situated in a variety of different camps that have traditionally been called the three solitudes — Business, Government and the Universities.

I am a businessman by trade, as President and Chief Executive officer of the Quaker Oats Company of Canada Limited in Peterborough. My spouse teaches Canadian history at Trent University — a university of which I was also the Chairman of the Board. To those of you in academic life, that must pose some interesting political challenges, particularly in a city the size of Peterborough. My children are also on the road to being better educated than I was.

One of the advantages of living and working in a smaller city which also includes a university is that one develops a greater understanding of academic and community life.

This afternoon I would like to explore with you some of my views as a Chief Executive Officer of a corporation as well as an individual who has been involved in some form of university life for the last number of years. The obvious question is, what is really happening in the private sector and what are employers looking for in university graduates? The premise would seem to be that you and I are at opposing ends. Your role

33

is to educate students in the liberal education tradition and mine to hire specialists.

More than ever before, there is a critical need in Canada to rekindle the "intellectual elite." If you look at the historical perspective of the 1940s and 1950s in this country, many of our leaders could move comfortably from business to government to universities in a type of tripartite understanding of the Canadian identity. We produced, over the course of the Second World War and for ten years after, political leaders, university thinkers and business giants who could talk to each other about common goals.

Today, al most of you will likely agree, the quality of political leadership has declined, business leadership may become more narrow and self-serving and university academia a hodgepodge of opposing views — tenure and security, collegiality and unionization. The three solitudes are more isolated than ever before. *Government*, whether at the political level or within the bureaucracy, is not viewed by the public as having a very high value system or image compared to that of thirty or forty years ago.

Business today is on a market-driven, deregulated growth curve which may set priorities for economic growth ahead of such crucial concerns as the environment. *Universities* are unable to decide what role is really expected of them and academics are now too much caught up in the high degree of government funding, and as public employees too much concerned about job security. Universities, which traditionally have led changes in social thought and direction, are now following trends.

Are we educating students to think creatively, write well and speak with conviction today or are we trying to meet the needs that university administrations feel society wants?

One of the great dichotomies that exist today is that the "view from the top" of the Chief Executive Officer requires a different type of graduate from perhaps that of those who are doing the hiring. A president first notices a young graduate when he or she reads a recommendation or an analysis and, in fact, during the first year, the Chief Executive Officer may not have even met this graduate. The second time that a graduate comes to the attention of a Chief Executive Officer is in a presentation situation in which the graduate is proposing, or is part of a proposal team, verbally presenting a recommendation. Finally, at some later stage, the information that a young graduate has picked up at the university becomes important, but the first impression is, does he or she write well, present clearly and think problems out in a creative way?

From a President's perspective, what is looked for in graduates today as potential managers of companies is a solid, wide-ranging background in education and particularly liberal arts. The ability of people to think on their feet, argue their cases and have a deep understanding of what is happening to society at large is becoming increasingly important.

On the other hand, the view of a personnel manager, the individual who goes to the universities to interview, is sometimes at odds with those objectives because the personnel manager is essentially looking for specialists to fill a position. In many cases, those who have a specialized type of education, whether in the sciences or in business, will have initial employment advantages over those with a liberal arts education.

I have found it quite interesting, when following graduates through our company, that after a couple of years we have forgotten what type of degree the individual has as it becomes less important than performance on the job. The ability to rise above the group and to inject one's own personality and motivation and creativity on the company is more important than the specific university degree.

In Peterborough, with our easy access to Trent University, we have hired a number of undergraduate liberal arts graduates from that school. In tracking their records within The Quaker Oats Company, we find that after a number of years, they are doing as well or as perhaps even better than graduates with an MBA or post-graduate degrees in science.

Although it is more difficult for them to pass the entry level requirements in joining a company, students with a liberal arts background are more adequately trained to deal with the kind of societal changes that face business.

I find myself increasingly disappointed with universities which, as I mentioned earlier, have traditionally been on the leading edge of change. My feeling today is that universities are essentially followers in our society. Let me give you two examples. *Environment* is the leading concern in our society today and yet one hears little from the universities on this subject. *Ethics* in politics and in business is another excellent example. Universities essentially abandon the whole ethics area, certainly in the "free-swinging" sixties and seventies and in fact there is a good argument today that university teachers may not be the best people to teach the subject of ethics. The enquiring mind of a university student should be challenged with those kinds of social concerns that transcend both politics and business. In many cases, university graduates are more "small c" conservative than any preceding generation.

Perhaps because of economic circumstances, students are much more concerned about jobs, careers, the house in Toronto and indeed the BMW.

What concerns me today is that graduates are not prepared to take many risks. They have an essentially conservative outlook towards the kinds of decisions that must be faced today whether it be in business or in government.

Another concerning trend is that young people today are not prepared, outside their own careers, to spend part of their lives in social contribution in the community. It is very difficult to encourage young people, after a busy day at the office, to help out in social services and community boards. Many times the answers we get are "no, I have got my career to look after and my next priority is my family and

35

children." If we continue with this trend, it seems that we will have more of what has been commonly labelled "the me generation."

Faced with this "small c" conservatism and a "me generation" mentality, the environmental crisis which the world faces will not be solved. How can we balance rational sustained economic growth with the rapid deterioration of our environment?

Last year, when travelling in the Soviet Union, I had an opportunity to view a society that, through a total emphasis on economic growth for three generations, absolutely ignored the environment. The Soviets are now becoming concerned and, for the first time, bumper stickers are appearing reading "save our forests." We have lived through, since the Second World War, an industrial and economic growth at great expense to our resources and our environment. The legacy that we leave to the next generation is not a very bright prospect.

Universities today, particularly in liberal arts education, must focus the students' minds on the questions and concerns of the development of our society. Businessmen by nature are entrepreneurs and they will build the apartment building on a river if it makes economic sense, or cut down a forest. Government and the university must be a counterbalance to what I would define as a normal entrepreneurial instinct that business has to grow and develop. Somebody in this society must say "no, you can only cut down one tree in ten" or "no, you cannot build beside a river" because in generations to come the public may want to use that river. If students and graduates today are not thinking about the counterbalances to economic growth or what I would call partnership with sustained development, they are likely more conservative than I am and that disturbs me greatly.

Having spent a number of years as a governor of Trent University, I am decidedly concerned about the "civil servant" status of university academics and researchers. With eighty per cent of the funding from the government to universities, there is little opportunity to develop a kind of international or world-class expertise. For instance, in Ontario, government funding for high school students per person per year is $5,500. At the undergraduate level in university, that funding drops to $3,500. We spend 35% less for a first-year undergraduate student's education than for a high school student. At the very time when young people are opening their eyes to the opportunities of a university education, we in fact spend least on their teaching. First-year students should have the best professors to open up intellectual curiosity in a variety of program offerings.

Unfortunately, many universities have developed, over the last ten years, undergraduate so-called "business programs" that offer a student a degree of sorts. Business is not blind to this and in fact would much prefer the business degree at a post-graduate level with a more liberal education at the undergraduate level. I think it is time that we look at these job-directed undergraduate programs that have little standing in the business community. It is obviously a great risk as universities in many cases have relied on the undergraduate business or policy degrees to appeal to students. It has been my view that students should take a broadly based undergraduate education and, if they so desire, specialize at the graduate level.

This country has basically relied on a system of government grants to fund universities. With a free trade prospect now being debated, how can we compete with the United States, let alone the rest of the world, unless there is more private funding for our universities? Immigrants today from other parts of the world are well educated and may take advantage of some of the opportunities in Canada, if we as Canadians cannot compete. As businessmen, corporate and individual donations to universities on a percentage basis is well behind the U.S. If we are going to improve our university environment, alumni, business and foundations, we must put more money into our university system.

In some cases, parents who are well-to-do are sending their children to American universities at a cost of about $25,000 a year because they feel the young people receive a superior education and more individual attention. Clearly, the elitism associated with such a move could very well place our Canadian students and graduates as second class citizens when competing in Canada and externally.

Many of us in Anglophone Canada have great difficulty in coping with another language — French. How are we going to compete in a world-class environment if, as Canadians, particularly Anglophones, we have difficulty working in a language other than English?

Our undergraduate liberal arts education programs must redefine a clear course to put second language instruction back on the agenda. It is time to redefine liberal arts education in Canada, particularly at the undergraduate level.

Let me summarize. Undergraduate liberal arts education is under-funded. In fact we spend less educating undergraduates than we do high school students. The ability to write well, think clearly, and speak with conviction on a broad range of societal subjects is important for the future direction of business as it co-exists with our environment. Universities should be on the forefront of change and stimulation, rather than following trends. Environmental concerns are primary in people's minds today and universities have a responsibility to make students aware. Unfettered economic growth without the important environmental balance is disastrous for the world.

Finally, we have lost the sense of ethics and nowhere is it taught in any substantive way. University educators, because of substantial government funding, find themselves in a civil service mode. They should change their focus and concern about tenure and job security, collegiality, and university ˙ unionization to the primary calling of educating our students.

We all, in this tripartite association — business, government and universities — have much to learn. We all have a stake in developing Canada's future leaders.

Howard Clark

---

*STRENGTHS
AND
WEAKNESSES
OF LIBERAL EDUCATION :
A COMMENT*

When I was invited to be a commentator on Lise Bissonnette's address today, I must confess I hesitated somewhat. It's well known, I think, that when Lise Bissonnette addresses an issue, she usually does so, so brilliantly that all of the major points have been covered. I was a little concerned that there might not be very much left to say, so somewhat defensively I prepared a stand-by text and I'm pleased to find that at least some of it is still useful. What I would like to do is offer some general remarks first of all, then address the theme of the session, namely, strengths and weaknesses of liberal education, and then go on to say a little bit about what we're doing at Dalhousie at present.

If I continue on a somewhat defensive note, I suppose I should point out that my background is firstly that of a university administrator, a department head, a Vice-President, and a President over a twenty-three year period and that obviously makes me of pretty dubious ability to contribute to a session such as this. Secondly, my background is that of a scientist, a chemist, one who has been actively involved in research over many years and still is, in a narrow area of chemistry. As I was writing these notes down, I thought to myself, it really is interesting that in doing so, I'm showing a certain defensive reaction to the whole issue that we are discussing. I began to wonder why. Let me return to that a little bit later and at this point just comment that perhaps because of my scientific background, my understandings of liberal education may be somewhat different from some of yours.

The title of this conference is, "Who's Afraid of Liberal Education?" and it seems to me, we might start there. It's more than a hypothetical question and one well worth discussing. Who *is* afraid of liberal education? In my experience, and speaking generally of faculty in universities at present, the answer is, we all are. Let me illustrate that. In my last couple of years at the University of Guelph, we devoted a great deal of time and effort to the discussion of the nature and role of undergraduate education, liberal education. Now, we found that difficult enough to do in a large committee, but I was struck by the fact that twice we had very good long debates in Senate; they were, I felt, some of the best Senate debates that were held at Guelph in recent years. But on the other hand, I sensed that they generated a great deal of unease and discomfort among faculty members, faculty members from all parts of the University. The discussion of education, the discussion of the nature and objectives of education, the discussion of liberal education, disturbed them, made them uncomfortable, whether they came from the humanities, the social sciences or the natural sciences. I found the same thing at Dalhousie. We were recently discussing a very brief statement on undergraduate education in a committee and I was struck again by the fact that the same set of words produced, from the humanists, a very defensive reaction, a defense of the traditional values of education, a complete misinterpretation of what the natural scientists thought the statements were, and we had a considerable debate trying to arrive at some agreement on just what the set of words did mean, and we were all uneasy although we appreciated the debate. Now why is that? Why is it that we are all a little afraid of liberal education? Certainly I agree with a point made earlier that a prime reason is the enormous pressure to specialize, which largely comes from the sciences. This has pervaded not only the natural sciences but the social sciences, and even reaches into the humanities. The pressure to cover subject matter; the pressure to present material that is the most up-to-date that we can give students; the pressure to train people not just as scientists, not just as chemists or as physicists or geologists, but I've even been told by people in history department that they see it as their job in an honors programme to train historians. The pressure to specialize that comes from the fast explosion of knowledge and information is causing very subtle and very profound effects throughout the universities.

It seems to me that this discomfort that we feel comes also from the fact that we have no common view within the institution of what our educational objectives and goals really are, of what we're all about educationally at the undergraduate level. More importantly, we seldom even discuss it and when I stop to think about it, it really is remarkable to me that in all the time I've spent in universities, I can recall just a minimal amount of time devoted to discussion of what we are about educationally. Now, certainly, there are discussions at the departmental level but even there I think they tend to be about rules and regulations. There may be a little discussion at the faculty level, but in terms of any institutional debate, any agreement institutionally of what a university education is all about, of what a liberal education is, we just don't have it. It seems to me that this discomfort I've mentioned comes from those two things, the specialization and the lack of institutional integrity, if you like, of leadership, if you wish, in fostering some sense, *any* sense, of what educationally the institution is about.

The intent today, as I understood it, is to say something about the strengths and weaknesses of liberal education at present. So let me just comment very briefly on strengths, because I think it is important to point out that we do have strengths at the present time and should not be totally defensive. Firstly, I think we all have no difficulty in agreeing that the very heart and soul of any university lies in the arts and science faculties, that they are the core of the university and that when you look at most universities in Canada or in North America, the vigour and strength of the intellectual life in those faculties at present is not too bad. It could be better, but it's certainly not disastrous. While that remains so, it's hard to believe that educationally we are doing a particularly bad job. Most surveys, from students and others, show that we are doing reasonably well, although I do think that the effects of specialization, the lack of coherence and common understanding of what we're trying to achieve is slowly eroding the effectiveness of what we are doing.

Secondly, in terms of strengths, it's worth looking at what people say about our graduates. Some of you, I am sure, have read the report of the Corporate Higher Education Forum "Making the Match" which is a good study of how business, the private sector, responds to university graduates. The general conclusion is quite favorable. It was interesting, as has already been mentioned, that we get very different perceptions from C.E.O.s than from those who do the hiring in the personnel department. That, I think, is more a commentary on the private sector than it is on the universities. Nevertheless, overall, the view is we're not doing too bad a job. But to my mind the weaknesses that we have at present are substantial and are certainly steadily outweighing the strengths.

Let me now list two or three weaknesses in relation to liberal education. To me, one of the most notable weaknesses of liberal education is, if you like, its complete lack of visibility within the university. Not only do we not quite know what liberal education is, we do essentially nothing to convey to our students some integrated sense of what's it's all about. Those of us in faculties of arts and science, certainly in the past few years, have been talking, I think perhaps a little smugly, about the virtues and qualities of the liberal education we provide, but where do we really explain to the student, where do we tell the student what a liberal education is all about? When I look through university calendars, which are the official documents that students use to try to steer themselves about in the university world, and look for some statement of the educational philosophy of a program, particularly a B.A. or a B.sc. in virtually every case, the calendar starts off with about a twenty-page list of totally incompehensible regulations and no statement of educational objectives or philosophy.

Secondly, and here I think I may differ somewhat from some of our previous speakers, to me a very major and profound weakness in what we are doing at the present is our inability to provide our students with a meaningful education which genuinely draws together the natural sciences and the social sciences and the humanities. To me, it is just a disgrace that we continue to produce graduates in the natural sciences whose exposure to the humanities and languages is minimal, and perhaps even more disgraceful that anyone can graduate from a university without some reasonable understanding of natural science and the scientific method. Whatever a liberal education is, it surely encompasses some concept of breadth, a breadth of understanding of the human experience, a sense of wholeness. And in an age when, whether we like it or not, science and technology increasingly influence our lives, we cannot give the sense of wholeness without exposure to a basic education in what science is all about. In my opinion, the most profound challenge that the universities face now is not to reassert the importance of a traditional liberal education, it's not to go back to the great books, it's not to define a list of the most recent great books, but to develop an understanding of what the new liberal education must be for the future. Surely, we should be looking forward, not backward, and surely that new liberal education has to contain, must be based on, some integrated view of the human experience in a technological world. We need to be debating the new liberal education, not the old.

Now, let me briefly comment on what we have been trying to do at Dalhousie. It has been my personal conviction for a number of years that the most central problem that universities face at present has nothing to do with money but is essentially the lack of coherence, the lack of agreement, the lack of a sense of purpose of what we are trying to do at the undergraduate level. Because of that, last September, I announced at Dalhousie (and I announced it to a convocation which we hold for first-year students, not in Senate) — I announced to the students that we were going to make undergraduate education at Dalhousie a priority over the next five years and that we would deliberately try to take steps to reform, change, improve the quality of undergraduate educational experience that our students receive. That we would try to put in place such measures that, after five or six years, we could look critically at what we had achieved. Now, you might well ask, what happens when a President stands up and says that? Well, the usual thing. There's a resounding thud. Not too much happens, at least initially, and I think it was certainly greeted with a large degree of skepticism and certainly with a comment from many that we could do very little without more money. We decided that we would proceed by holding a symposium and the symposium would be in the spring, in early March, but that prior to the symposium which was carefully planned, we would do an extensive amount of survey work trying to assess and get an accurate set of measures of faculties, students, parents, alumni opinions of undergraduate education at Dalhousie. I won't go into great detail, but there certainly are a lot of things that come out of that research that support many of the things that were listed earlier as being the major obstacles to educational reform in the universities. First of all, it is clear that when one tries to talk about under-graduate education in the university, it tends almost inevitably to be converted to teaching. How do we teach? Yet, undergraduate education is what the student experiences, not what the faculty member does. And yet, all the time, we are finding that there is this continuing tendency to convert a discussion of undergraduate education into one of teaching and how to improve teaching. Secondly, we have for that very reason tried to focus on undergraduate education and on the students. What does the student experience? What does the student experience when he or she comes to university, what does he or she think on leaving the university, what has the educational experience done for them? Our students provided many comments about our education, and on the whole reported that it was of good quality, but there were some other interesting points. For example, students certainly felt that faculty members should be more accessible and should be more available for talking to undergraduate students. But it is interesting that in response to the questionnaire that went to faculty members containing questions about how they would like their time distributed, an overwhelming majority obviously wanted to be devoting less time to teaching and more time to research. There were very, very disturbing differences between the students' expectations and hopes, and the hopes and intentions of the faculty members. I think that issue is one that needs a great deal of very serious debate.

The symposium in March started on a Thursday and ran through to Saturday morning, and in organizing it, the planning committee adopted a very significant ploy. They wrote to every department and asked every department to appoint two delegates, the intention being that those two delegates should attend the symposium and report back to the departments on everything that happened in the symposium. That ensured that we had at least two faculty members from every department present. Without that, I think, there's no question but that the audience would have been much smaller! Nevertheless, it was interesting to me that we started on the Thursday morning with nine hundred to a thousand people there and we finished at noon on Saturday with virtually the same number. They were all there and it was interesting talking to faculty members going over on the Thursday, one or two of whom I know quite well as friends, who pointedly told me that they had been chosen as delegates by the department and supposed they should attend, but would far rather be back in their labs. When I saw them on Friday and Saturday, they had heard so many controversial

43

things that they felt they had to come back and argue and stay, and they did. The interest in the symposium was particularly high.

It's worth commenting also that we looked hard for a keynote speaker and I was disappointed that although we searched high and low we really didn't feel that we could find the sort of speaker within Canada that we could have hoped to find. We finally invited J. Kayser, from M.I.T. Some of you might well question M.I.T.'s role in relation to liberal education but it is interesting that a philosopher holds the title of Vice-Dean of Undergraduate Studies at M.I.T. His comments really stimulated an enormous amount of discussion. I won't attempt to go through them but they were relevant because M.I.T. is engaged on a project to completely reform undergraduate education at M.I.T. However, they have recognized that to make progress, and to have a significant change, it will take them a minimum of ten years. I think that supports Lise Bissonnette's remarks in terms of the complexity of trying to bring about change within the complex organization that a university represents. The symposium, as I said, was very successful but then, one asks, what comes after that? We have had a committee working, over the summer, pulling together everything that has come out of the symposium and there are already a number of very significant things happening. But it seems to me, from all of the discussions that we are having, that there are two major areas of difficulty. One is to get faculty to accept that what one is talking about is undergraduate education, not teaching; that education goes on not just in the classroom; that the university offers a total experience to the student and that the university needs to be concerned with that total experience. There is just an enormous tendency to concentrate on teaching in the classroom and to narrow down undergraduate education to that narrow view. Far greater than that problem, however, is the curriculum problem. How do you get any movement within the university in terms of a curriculum which will be a genuine new liberal education for a technological age? J. Kayser made one comment that struck me as particularly important. He made the point that there had been, in his opinion, three historic events in history; one was the movement from a nomadic existence to agriculture, one was the discovery of and all the things that followed from metallurgy, and the third historic event, which he was asserting we're experiencing now, is the marriage of science, technology and management. He went on to say that, if that is the case, perhaps the most difficult thing that we have to do in education is to find means of making connections between science, technology, the humanities, ethics, values, and the arts, (certainly M.I.T. is approaching it in that way) and trying to devise means of making connections between those areas slowly over time, to introduce courses and programs that integrate them over a ten-year period.

Finally, it seems to me that we are not just talking about liberal education, we are not just talking about what the new liberal education should be for the future. To my mind, in many senses, what we are talking about is the survival of the universities, because I really believe that if we cannot in the next period of time arrive at a much clearer institutional consensus (and I believe it has to be done at the institutional level), of what we are about educationally, the pressures of specialization will overwhelm us and universities as we now know them, and certainly the historic concept of the university will be nothing other than a concept and something of the past. I really believe that's what we are talking about. Now, it may be that specialization is going to overwhelm us whether we like it or not. If that's the case, I suppose one may have to say, "so be it," but on the other hand, why do we just sit there and let it happen? Why aren't we talking about it and why aren't we debating what a university is and should be? Why aren't we conducting those essential intellectual debates about the educational purpose of the university, which are surely at the heart of the institution? If I can do nothing more, I would hope that, at least at Dalhousie, even if we go down in flames, we've at least debated some of the issues. I would encourage all of you to try to do the same.

Charles Karelis

*GENERAL EDUCATION
CURRICULUM TRENDS
IN
THE UNITED STATES*

I am going to try just to talk descriptively for a while about American trends or U.S. American trends in the higher education curriculum and particularly the general education curriculum. There is a sort of ticking that one hears as you listen to the curriculum debate to your south. The question I want to ask is : Is this the ticking of a pendulum moving meaninglessly back and forth or is it the ticking of a time bomb about to explode into what Alan Bloom calls a crisis at the peaks of learning or an intellectual crisis of our civilization? That's one way of asking my question.

First of all, let me be clear over what the debate is about : it's about what in our terms, in U.S. American terms, is called general education, which is to say the part of the undergraduate curriculum that lies outside of the major. It normally comes before the major, although that's probably not true by definition, it is required of all students and it is non-specialized. So what is at issue? The main point is that this is a debate about means and about ends; it's about what general education should try to accomplish and it's about the kind or type of general education that will best serve those ends.

Let me start with ends. General education reminds me a little bit of what Nietzsche said about the ancient practice of punishment, which is that even the people who believe in it don't agree about what it's for. In fact Ernest Boyer and Art Levine did a useful survey of statements about general education made around the First World War, the Second

World War and in the present day — the three great moments of revival in general education — and they discern more than twenty different purposes that have been ascribed to general education in these three periods. About six of the twenty purposes have been urged in all three periods. (1) General education, so say its advocates, is needed so that mankind can share its common heritage with new generations. (2) It's needed for the preserving of democracy. (This was most often cited, incidentally, in the decade after 1945). (3) General education is seen in all three periods as being needed for improving students' morality, particularly making them less selfish. (4) A fourth aim has been said to be that of integrating diverse groups into a larger society. This relates closely of course to the first aim, which is that of integrating new generations into the community of those who have lived before. We could talk, perhaps, about longitudinal and cross-sectional integration. (5) A fifth stated aim of general education has been overcoming undue educational specialization. Even though this seems kind of obvious it's worth pointing it out, that general education is often said to be general not only in the sense of being essential for all but also in the sense of being broad in its focus. You can see logically that one could have one without the other. (6) General education has been ascribed the purpose of overcoming the vocationalist mind-set and the career orientation of students, a point which entails that general education is to be liberal rather than directly practical.

My point in ticking all these off is simply, again, to point out that they differ, that the different believers in a non-specialized required foundational curriculum in the U.S. have wanted to put this curriculum to different uses. Even where there has been some agreement, the purposes have often been ranked differently, with one advocate giving first place to the sharing of the great tradition and another caring less about that and more about making sure that all students have had a common intellectual experience of some sort. In sum, believers in general education in the U.S. have not spoken with a single voice, and in addition there have been plenty of straight-out opponents. So the allies don't agree among themselves, and there's also a bunch of people who don't agree with the idea of general education at the undergraduate level for whatever aim; and there's an even larger number of people who find it convenient to advocate the name but who oppose the thing itself.

Now, working from my admittedly limited sense of where the debate is at in Canada at the moment, I thought it might be good to focus at least at the outset on this broad brush issue : why have general education at all with any of these aims? I think that I want to characterize the American attitude or the U.S. American attitude here as ambivalent. There is ambivalence on the desirability of general education, it's old and it's deep and it is one aspect of an old identity crisis in the very soul of U.S. higher education. Like many other identity crises, this one goes back to the question of which of two parents deserves the deeper loyalty. As has often been noted, U.S. higher education sprang from the marriage of the English and continental secondary school on the one hand, and the German university on the other hand. There were also a number of other significant but ultimately less significant inputs such as the agricultural trade school and more recently the social service agency, which I think has had a bit of input into the community college system. But the main parents I think are the ones that I mentioned, and each of these, the English and continental secondary schools and the German university, bequeaths a view of general education to the offspring, the American college and university. In the English and continental secondary schools, of course, virtually the whole curriculum was required with few electives up until the very end. Moreover, most of the six perennial aims that I talked about were ascribed to this curriculum: it was broad, it was non-vocational, it bestowed a uniform educational experience, it passed on the great traditions and perhaps above all, it aimed to shape values and moral beliefs or at least, it aimed to shape deportment — manners if not morals. By contrast, the German university tradition ignored general education altogether, focusing instead on specialized, scholarly and professional education for the elite, especialy for future civil servants. The general education of the German bureaucrat and professional man had already taken place before he got to university, in the Gymnasium.

Now, insofar as American universities, particularly such as Johns Hopkins, Clark and Chicago, were modeled on this German ideal, they prided themselves on the research achievements of faculty in separate departments rather than on the teaching vocation of collaborating colleagues. As for the idea that the faculty were responsible for moral education, this was, for these descendants, largely rejected as verging on the realm of the ineffable and the irrational. Real scholars dealt in provable facts. A modern representative of this viewpoint was heard to dismiss general education recently as "freshman thought." So one source of hostility to general education in the U.S. college has been the fact the U.S. college has important roots in the German university.

Another source of hostility has been outside the university itself in the characteristic individualism of U.S. Americans, first noted in the early 19th century by Alexis de Tocqueville. U.S. citizens are supposedly stubbornly unique, this is the strength of America, the source of its creativity and its competitiveness. Accordingly, there is no sense whatever in running all our undergraduates through the very same sequence of courses. This was in fact the view of Harvard College's great post Civil War President Charles William Eliot, who in 1869 abolished the lock step curriculum which had come down from colonial days and replaced it with a system of free electives. He sought, as one writer put it, to free students and faculty, to introduce new subjects, offer advanced work, pursue scholarship and scientific research. Students would have under this elective system the freedom to develop their particular talents and interests. This is the individualist source, if you will, of the hostility to general education. Almost exactly a century later, in the 1960s, history was to repeat itself but this time with a sour twist. By the late 1960s, most colleges had some kind of general education program in place. Once again, the elective system of Eliot and his progeny had been replaced, as the pendulum had swung back, by a kind of general education, but once again, the individualist impulse arose to challenge these programs and to demand more elective freedom for students. But this time, individualism was a negative force, not a positive one. It had to do not with releasing creative energy à la Eliot but with doing one's own thing, with thumbing one's nose at society, at the older generation, at authority all conveniently symbolized by the tradition of the university. When people say that there's a revival of general education today, well, I guess there is but you've got to remember it's against the backdrop of this anarchy that the current developments appear as a revival of general education. I'm going to argue that they're not all that much of a revival unless you compare them to what was left after the 1960s.

One last source of enmity to general education is cited by Professor Alan Bloom in his recent bestseller *The Closing of the American Mind*. This is the nervousness which U.S. intellectuals are alleged to feel about saying that some things, especially some books, are better and/or truer than others. According to Bloom, the U.S. academy is in the grips of epistemological relativism, a view that knowledge of all kinds is conditional on the characteristics of the knower and particularly on the race, class and gender of the knower. As Bloom traces the logic, it follows that there is no hope of identifying a set of books or courses that are just plain true or just plain influences for the good. Indeed, still on the relativist view, the traditional idea that there are just plain true and good books obtained only because the academics making the calls have been traditionally members or at least servants of one class, one race and one gender. From the relativist standpoint, Bloom argues, the democratization and diversification of the student body and the faculty (and it is a demonstrable fact that there has been a diversification of a student body and a faculty during the sixties and seventies has inevitably exposed the traditional great works curriculum or great books curriculum as the hidden agenda of a special interest group.

Of course, Bloom's answer to all this is that the premise is false, relativism is false, it is a wrong epistemology; some things are better than others and can be known to be better than others. The real hidden agenda for Bloom is that of the irrationalist counter-culture left over from the sixties, and a left left over from the sixties, which simply wants to unseat the reigning gods and put false gods in their place so that they can kick out the old high priests of learning and become high priests of learning themselves. That is Bloom's version of what's happening, and hence, his talk about the curricular debate as an intellectual crisis of our civilization.

Now, what I've been trying to convey is that general education in the U.S. university has been part of several debates at once. A debate over whether universities should be trying to form the whole person for that person's various roles on the one hand, or training professionals according to the German University idea for particular roles on the other hand. A debate over whether or not universities should be trying to unify our culture longitudinally and cross-sectionally. A debate about the validity of individualism. And finally it has been part of a debate about the very possibility of objective knowledge.

The next question, plainly, is who is winning these debates and what are the concrete implications for the U.S. curriculum. As I look at the colleges that I'm familiar with, as I read other people's surveys of the scene, and as I study the grant applications we get at my grant-making agency, my view would be that, in most places, the various debates are at an impasse. Neither side has achieved clear victory and each side is capable of embarrassing the other side publicly with a forceful presentation of its own position. As a consequence, most colleges are struggling to do something about general education without exposing themselves too much to the jibes of the opponents. You've therefore got a situation of people wanting to move forward cautiously, fending off the jibes of the opponents on each of these various debates. The compromise that is being reached, the compromise that is commonest, looks something like this.

First of all, the pro general education view is winning on the specialization issue and on the vocationalism issue. You've got the vocationalism kind of principle on the run and likewise specialization, but there's more — not only is a requirement of broad liberal study being strongly endorsed around the United States, typically there is also support for the idea that it is essential for all students to know certain things. Again this is a distinction I've tried to make before, it's not just some broad liberal knowledge that's being insisted on but a particular body of liberal knowledge. The feeling is that you haven't really been to college unless you know certain things. That's all going the way of the general education people, that part of it, but just when you think you know what's happening, it veers off in another direction. Just when you might expect to hear, on the heels of what I've said, an endorsement of the classical great works plus Western history curriculum, the reasoning of the typical American faculty member veers off in another direction entirely.

The broad liberal learning that is being demanded is not the mastery of certain content, it is the mastery of either certain skills, like critical thinking or writing, or certain so-called ways of knowing like the way of knowing that is allegedly peculiar to historians or the way of knowing that is allegedly peculiar to literary critics or biologists. So again, general education at the typical U.S. campus is now to be an education not in content but in skills and modes of knowing. This, I think, is the heart of the compromise between the two philosophies I laid out before. On the one hand, the compromise position does grant that it is important for all students to achieve broad learning, but on the other hand, the compromise escapes the relativist charge of cultural chauvinism by remaining content-neutral. It ducks on content, and not

51

only does it escape the charge that the relativist position makes by ducking on content, but as a practical matter, it enables the specialized departments to continue with business as usual. Nothing has to change because the students are now supposed to pick their courses from an existing pool: some humanities courses, to find out how humanists think, some social science courses, to find out how social scientists think, some natural science courses and so on.

Now again, this is a generalization and not every general education program in the U.S. conforms to this model. But Boyer and Levine, who surveyed the field within the last decade, concluded that it was, at least when they did their survey, a very safe generalization indeed. About 95% of all colleges and universities, they say, base their general education programs, at least in part, on a study of selected courses within these traditional academic departments and divisions; and they mean humanities, social science, natural science. Now, I've got two annotations. First, when Boyer and Levine say that general education programs are distribution requirements at least in part, one may wonder what the other part is. Well, the other part of the typical general education program varies from place to place. It doesn't vary all that much but it varies. For one thing, many U.S. colleges are so dissatisfied with the basic academic skills of their incoming freshmen that they require courses in how to write and how to compute, and they call these catch up courses part of general education. Even Harvard, you know, on top of its other general education requirements, has something called writing, you've got to learn to write. Beside these remedial things that get thrown in and called general education, a number of colleges in the U.S. are trying to respond to the public perception that American college graduates are (a) xenophobic and (b) professionally unethical, by patching in requirements relating to international study on the one hand and professional ethics on the other. That's the first annotation, that's what I mean by "at least in part." The second thing is this: Boyer and Levine say that students are typically required to choose among selected, that's their word, selected courses in each of the traditional divisions — humanities, social sciences and natural sciences. The point here is that typically not every humanities course that is in the college catalogue will satisfy the distribution requirement for humanities, not every social science course will satisfy the distribution requirement for social sciences and so on. For example, at Harvard, which has a modified form of this system, there are 185 courses that can be taken to satisfy the general education requirement out of more than 1 000 courses in the catalogue, so you've got a limited pool. During the last incarnation of general education at Harvard, the idea was that almost anything would do and you got Swedish cinema and the films of John Ford and current health care crisis and so on. But not now. Now there's an approved pool of courses, it tends obviously to be courses of the introductory level, that's kind of obvious, but there's more, often there are other criteria such as whether a course stresses the methodology of the discipline. Because after all, we're learning to learn, right, so we need to not only be shown how historians think, but we need to be told, this is how historians think, notice how historians think so that later you too can think as historians even though you don't know anything about the past. Now, only a few colleges limit the pool of eligible general education courses to traditional survey courses.

You might ask, why is that, what happened to the good old survey course? Well, going back to my hypothesis that today's general education programs are compromises between these two very different views of higher education, the old survey course has disappeared for two reasons : (a) it made too many disputable commitments about what societies, what books, what people, what philosophies, are essential for students to know about and (b) it diverted too much faculty time from specialized teaching in the disciplines. With the new model, by contrast, the specialized course can actually count as a general education course at the same time as long as it's methodologically self-conscious and so on. So both ideals of higher education can be served at once. However, I hasten to add, lest I seem merely to move on a political plane here, that there is another explanation for the disappearance of the survey course as well as the one I have just given, and this explanation is very different. It says that the survey is disappearing because the survey course is out of tune with the latest research in pedagogy. The survey course is said to be predicated on the notion that students learn well passively in large lectures where they're expected to memorize what they're told and spoon it back on the final exam. This explanation goes on to say that this is now known to be false, this is not how students learn, students learn better and learn more when they participate in small seminars. The old survey course is therefore gotten rid of for that reason. Moreover, and this is crucial for this explanation of the disappearance of the survey course, mere information goes out of date so rapidly that what students really need to keep up in a fast changing world is to learn how to learn. They need to learn how to evaluate, learn how to analyze and for this general education stressing intellectual skills is much more valuable than survey courses stressing the acquisition of content.

So here we have two quite different accounts of what's happened to the old survey course, one explanation in terms of the politics of the academy and another explanation in terms of the prevailing pedagogical theory. There is, I might add, stealing here from E.D. Hirsch's book about cultural literacy, some irony in all this because back in the 19th century, the study of the classical languages was thought to be particularly good for disciplining and training the mind. If students could master their declensions and conjugations and compose in the manner of Virgil, then they could keep up in a fast changing world, they would have learned how to think. Along came a 20th century psychologist called Thorndike who did some experiments that discredited this idea of transferable skills and helped to kill the study of the classics. Subsequent work by psychologists has continued to cast doubt on the idea of content-neutral powers of reasoning transferable beyond the original subject matter. Hence, it is perhaps paradoxical to hear content-neutral skills being invoked again, this time, in defense of a curriculum that is poles apart from the classical curriculum of a century ago. If the thinking-skills defense of the classical curriculum is empirically inadequate, one might have thought it should also be inadequate as a defense of the distribution requirement curriculum which is at the oposite end of the spectrum.

So far, I've been just generalizing. Let me now look at a couple of specific examples. The first one is at Harvard and it was voted in after considerable discussion in the mid-1980s. It replaced a general education program that simply required a few courses in the three divisions and which more or less could be satisfied by anything in the catalogue. The new program, the mid-eighties one, has several key provisions, and let me tell you what they are. First of all, the old three-part categorization of the humanities, the natural and the social sciences has been replaced. Now, students must take courses in each of five areas. First, three courses must be taken in literature and the arts together; two courses must be taken in history; the third is that two courses must be taken in something called social analysis and moral reasoning; fourth, two courses must be taken in science; and fifth, one course must be taken in foreign cultures. The first thing is therefore that there is now a five-way division replacing the three-way division. Second, the pool of courses that can be chosen from, in order to satisfy each of the divisional requirements is, as I said before, much smaller. Each course is included in the pool not for its coverage of a particular subject matter, but now for its capacity to introduce students to a particular way of thinking.

Plainly then, Harvard fits well within the mainstream of general education programs in the U.S. today. It is called a core curriculum, indeed it calls itself a core curriculum, but as my former boss Secretary Bennett said in a controversial speech, it is really more of a symbolic nod in the direction of a core or, in his much-quoted allusion to the popular beer from Colorado, it is core light. Harvard reaffirms the principle that every student should know certain things, but in practice, there are no particular courses that each student has to take, there are no particular books that each student has to read, no particular countries he or she has to study, no great figures or events each must be acquainted with. You can graduate without having read a single Greek tragedy, without having read a single Shakespearean play, without having read Hobbes, Locke, Rousseau, Marx or Mill, without ever having seen a picture by Rubens, Rembrandt or Picasso, without ever having studied the French, American or Russian revolutions and some students do exactly that, so it is core light.

My second example is called the Miami plan for liberal education. It's now evolving in Miami University, a big and very good public university in Oxford, Ohio. Let me just get directly to what I want to say about it. The basic scheme again is that each student has to satisfy a set of distribution requirements and, as at Harvard, the old tripartite division is being replaced by a more elaborate framework. This one is a little more idiosyncratic. Each student is required to take at least three courses in a category called fine arts, history and humanities. This means you can avoid, for instance, history and just take fine arts and the humanities if you want to. Parenthetically, they admit that you can graduate without even having taken any literature. Then, there is a requirement of three courses in either physical or biological science, a requirement of at least one course in math or technology, then three courses in a category known as social science and world cultures. Indeed, within social science and world cultures the requirement is for a least one course in each so students can escape the study of Western culture but not the study of non-Western culture. Again, not just any social science or physics or biology course will satisfy the requirements. There is a limited pool, as at Harvard, but in this case, Miami tries to spell out in much more detail what makes a course in social science or physics or biology count as a liberal or general education course. First of all, it has to nurture a student's powers of analysis, that's an uncontroversial example of the general education as intellectual skills business, but then they go on to stipulate that eligible courses must also promote the view that gender, race and class condition our understanding.

So now the view is not that our gender and our race and our class may affect our beliefs if we're not careful to be objective, which would be something that would be not controversial surely, but rather that the world is a different place depending on where you see it from. This is what a course must actually argue to be eligible to satisfy the proposed general education requirement in Miami. The relativist epistemology functions in Miami not only as an obstacle to the acceptance of a common curriculum; it is actually being promoted as one of the great truths that the liberal arts have to teach. As to whether one's acceptance of the relativist epistemology itself is conditioned by one's gender, race and class or whether relativism is somehow a non-relative truth, on this question the architects of the Miami plan have so far been silent. There is no mention of Plato, Hume or any of the other guys that didn't agree with that. Here, in any event, we have a second example of what I've been calling the mainstream approach to general education in the U.S., namely, distribution requirements plus a limited pool of courses that can be used to fulfill them.

I have been trying to describe the mainstream view of general education on campus, but a major point that I want to make is that it is very questionable whether the typical academic idea of general education in the U.S. reflects the views of the average layman. When average educated people in the U.S. think about what it is that all college students ought to know, they probably have something like the traditional Western civ. curriculum in mind, the standard Western literary and philosophical classics plus the basic facts of Western history. I think that the academic culture in the U.S. may be somewhat at odds on the subject of general education with the larger society. My main evidence of this is the phenomenal popular success of Alan Bloom's book *The Closing of the American Mind.* We are talking about a hard-cover book being on the bestseller list for 52 or so weeks and then becoming a bestseller in soft cover, along with diet books and health books. We are talking about a book that has been editorialized about, has been discussed on T.V. talk shows week after week, and I think that Bloom's book has to be one of the best-selling books on the college curriculum in American history. So, again, it's enormously popular, but not only is Bloom's prescription being followed by only 5 or 10% of American colleges, but as far as one can tell, the book is hardly even getting serious attention at the other 90 or 95%. For instance, the keynote speaker at this year's conference of one of the major U.S. higher education association was billed as reacting to Bloom. In fact, in the first paragraph of his speech he dismissed the book, admitted that he hadn't finished it and was rewarded with an appreciative laugh from the assembled academics before he turned to other matters. I think that this may be a sort of symbol of the reaction to the Bloom book on American campuses.

So, there is a division in the U.S. between the academy and the larger public on the subject of general education. The next question is why? I've already talked about the campus perspective, the power of the scholarly specializations and relativistic suspicion of anything resembling a canon. Is the public perception, then, just a mirror image of this? On the part of the academy, you have the specialization and the suspicion of the canon. Is it juxtaposed to a preference for the big picture plus an exaggerated trust in the wisdom of the dead white males who wrote the classics? Is that what's going on — the public just trusting these dusty old people? I hope it isn't because I think there is a better and more liberal case for the traditional great books curriculum, one that sees it not as a museum for received wisdom, not as a way for students to avoid wrestling with life's great issues for themselves, but rather as a debate or indeed the great debate on life's perennial questions.

On the centrality of God, read the Bible and then read the greatest English author, Shakespeare, for whom God is a virtual irrelevancy. On the nobility of the warrior, read Homer and then read Eric Maria Remarque. On the sanctity of property, read Locke and then Marx. On the virtues of democracy, Jefferson and then Plato. On women, Virginia Woolf and then Schopenhauer and so on. What we have in the standard authors, then, is hardly the smug consensus depicted by the critics. It is rather a series of confrontations that must challenge students to acknowledge the superficiality of their own intuitive ways of framing the alternatives, that must open up their survey of their own life options.

Having said that, we may grant that the mainstream view, the skills view, has got hold of a corner of the truth at least. An education in critical thinking skills and in moral reasoning is arguably necessary in order for students to weigh and choose among the great visions, in order for them to resist the literary charms of say Plato, or the dry emotion-alism of a Remarque. But how can intellectual skills possibly be sufficient? Surely one could spend a lifetime engaged in critical thinking without hitting on the Homeric ideal for oneself or, for that matter, the ideal of Jane Austen. Surely one could have mastered moral analysis without being remotely able to imagine the great range of lifestyles that have been characterized as virtuous by men and women across the generations. The point is that students should not be condemned to make their life choices in a vacuum, devoid of real, exciting and well argued options. They need exposure to the great debates.

Here we need to be honest about how this approach would strike the people we've been calling the campus mainstream. I think that they might worry that even if the great works can be seen as a debate, even if there is no smug consensus among them, still there is a sort of dogmatism present. The dogmatism is not at the first level but at the second, a dogmatism not about which way of living is the worthiest, or which interpretation of the human condition is the truest, or which form of social organization is the most efficient and just but nevertheless a dogmatism about which alternatives are worth taking seriously. Who is to say whom the great debate is among? Isn't it interesting that when living, white, establishment males identify the key partisans it's always dead, white, establishment males that they identify? It is along these lines that the sceptics object to the great books curriculum, even seen as a great debate, much less as the repository of wisdom. Nor will it do simply to mumble something about the test of time and pretend that the sceptics should sink back in defeat. For the test of time, the famous test of time, is itself doubly biased, isn't it? Only certain races and classes and genders have been in a position to produce works of art, literature and philosophy in the first place, and secondly, the jury, the cultural elites that get to say what is and what isn't a classic, is itself composed largely of one race, one class, one gender. Surely then, certain viewpoints must have been excluded from this great debate of ours.

I'm afraid that I'm going to stop without trying to resolve the question of whether there is dogmatism in the choice of combatants in our great debate. My own personal view, for what's it's worth, is that there isn't. After all, it is the agents of the business classes that have put Marx on everybody's short list of classics. It is the social establishment that has elevated 100 anti-establishment satires to the same status, nor have many so-called neglected classics, the things that are allegedly left out by the test of time, survived the first flush of some journalist's enthusiasm to earn lasting stature. For my money, the test of time seems largely a good test.

Before finishing, let me just review quickly what I have said. What I've been trying to do is to give you a U.S. perspective, perhaps an idiosyncratic U.S. perspective, on the great struggle towards a reformed general education curriculum. I've talked about its various purposes, its friends and its enemies, and the compromise that they have reached in the United States. Finally, I suggested that the general public may not support this compromise. I have suggested that this may not be due to dogmatism or indifference but to a popular understanding that students need exposure to a wide range of options, of visions, of philosophies before they can make their personal and political choices responsibly. I hope all this may be of some use to you as you set about the great reform task on which you are now launched.

Adrian Marriage

THEORICAL IMPEDIMENTS,
PRACTICAL DIFFICULTIES
AND
ONE ENCOURAGING CASE

I imagine I was invited to take part in this conference principally on account of my long association with UBC's Arts One programme, and hence that it was supposed I would use this forum chiefly to talk about that programme. I started out in an attempt to satisfy those expectations, but I quickly discovered that the subject remained inert at the purely descriptive level and that it only took on life when it was used to point towards and to instantiate questions of a general character. Or rather, I discovered that as a case study it would only take on theoretical resonance when it was treated at a level of descriptive detail which was quite beyond my resources of time, both in the delivery of the paper and in its preparation. I am convinced, as it happens, that one of our unmet needs in the study of education is the maintenance of a strong literature of case studies; partly because it is a field which seems irresistibly to invite premature schematization, requiring the world's sheer untidiness as a corrective, and partly because — as David Riesman remarked many years ago — we just don't know enough about such elementary matters as who actually makes the decisions in the very universities where we profess the subject. But this, I judge, is not the time or place for an exercise which looks modest and turns out to be intolerably ambitious. Instead, I have sought and obtained the permission of the conference organizers to circulate a brief formal account of Arts One, to which I would merely append the conventional phrase "Further details available on request."

Meanwhile, I will devote myself today to questions less circumscribed by the circumstances of their origin; though at every point in what I say I shall be drawing upon my experiences in Arts One, as well as in the tragically short-lived and meteorically brilliant Experimental College Programme in Berkeley during the mid-1960s.

I need to begin with a brief prefatory statement about the terms of reference. In this paper I shall be using the term "liberal education" in preference to the term "general education," although the two are often used interchangeably nowadays and it is the latter which chiefly figures in the conference programme. "General education," in my view, is a residual term, taking its meaning from what it does *not* denote : that is, loosely put, it is whatever we think it is we have in mind when we are not speaking about a B.A. in Classical Studies or a Ph.D. in Economics. I am sure that this marks out a genuinely important area of educational concern, but I am equally sure that it is not the set of concerns to which we are directed by an interest in liberal education. Under certain conditions a general education might well do the work of a liberal education. But it is also possible that under other conditions a degree taken in six subjects rather than one, or even no subject in particular, would simply produce an illiberal dilettante rather than an illiberal specialist. It is in light of such a possibility, if for no other reason, that I want to insist on this distinction.

In any event, the organizers of the present conference have made an editorial decision to exclude from discussion any direct address to questions concerning the very nature of liberal education. I do not doubt, or I do not deeply and painfully doubt, for what it is worth to say so, that this was tactically shrewd. To the extent that such discussions were likely to have resolved themselves into a contest of definitions, proceeding in turn from assumptions too deep and inarticulate to make even disagreement useful, we are probably better off hoping to take the subject by indirection and stealth than by storming it in force. Two days are surely not enough for what anybody who has thought about the matter for more than two minutes must recognize is bound to be a long siege in an even longer campaign. At this stage of things, we can only hope that there will indeed be a campaign.

Yet having said this, somewhat redundantly affirming my agreement with an editorial decision to which I would have to submit in any case, I must immediately enter disclaimers and make discriminations. It is one thing to commend the expedient good sense of these topical constraints for a here-and-now occasion; it is another thing altogether to assume that they are forced upon us because they express something utterly intractable or quite irresolvable in the subject itself, so that there would *never* be an occasion on which it would be profitable to address the question directly, and therefore none on which we should have an obligation to address it : there being no duty to do what is useless. The decision to confine our attention over these two days to canvassing possibilities, analyzing obstacles and describing cases is a pragmatic deferment which can be justified readily enough. But it would have an unhappy effect indeed (however unintended) if it blunted our recognition of the fact that the task itself remains quite inescapable, enormously difficult, and altogether urgent; and that what serves to make it all those things is the answer that has to be given to the question which supplies the title to the conference. "Who's afraid of liberal education?" I fear we must reply, "A large number of people, for a large number of reasons." We deceive ourselves if we think otherwise. Whatever else needs to be said about the matter, I think we shall go nowhere unless we acknowledge that there are those who believe that it is idle to talk about liberal education and futile to attempt it, as well as others, very probably greater in number, who possess no ideas worth the name concerning what would be entailed either in the talk or the attempt. Nor, if the further truth be told, can it be said that these people are to be met exclusively in the memberships of lunatic fringes, philistine minorities and crudely sectarian lobbies, which is to say, however threatening an enemy, an enemy which is at least reas-suringly camped *outside* our gates. On the contrary, they are, in the contexts and for the purposes which interest us here, to be met mainly and significantly as members of —— pre-eminently as members of — what Carlyle called the articulate classes. The doubts are educated doubts, the arguments sophisticated arguments, and the tone of voice dismissive but cultivated. Yet this should not surprise us greatly. After all, it was Callicles and Thrasymachus and I.F. Stone that Socrates reckoned he had to take with intellectual seriousness; not some lout shouting abuse at him from the other side of the market place.

Now it is plain enough that I cannot hope in the few moments available to me to say very much about what this rejection of liberal education rests upon, whether the spirit of the rejection be more in sorrow than in anger or more in scorn than sorrow. Nor can I undertake to say how often it rests upon nothing at all, in the sense that it merely proceeds from special interests which use one argument or another (whatever lies to hand) to give themselves moral countenance. But I think I must say something to the purpose, first because it would be teasing to raise the subject but not pursue it at all, but more essentially because I am of the opinion that the greatest single impediment, or body of impediments, to liberal education is — for want of a better word — theoretical. Not all theories are explicit, of course; and indeed, in the kinds of forum in which the issue is likely to pose itself (a faculty curriculum committee, for example) I suspect one would be dealing with decidedly elliptical versions of the doctrines I am about to mention. Never-theless, something like the following, in my experience, can usually be either heard or plausibly inferred. (In strict sociological accuracy I should also include the numerous variations upon "'Shut up!' he explained." But perhaps those can be taken for granted).

I begin with the observation (not because any of us needs to be told but because my analysis requires that we remind ourselves of the fact) that the modern university, both as an engine of invention and discovery and as a focal point for our habits of civility, is one of the truly remarkable achievements of our era. Perhaps, indeed, there has never been an institution which so consistently succeeded in mobilizing so much human intelligence at such extraordinarily high levels of social organization to more potent and varied effect. These successes, *and the regularity with which they are achieved*, depend on many factors, not all of which could even be named; but it is quite clear that they hinge in the most essential way upon the working out and systematization of a minutely articulated division of labour in the activities of intellect. This division of labour, in its turn, generates the catalogues of disciplines and departments which describe the activities of the modern university and certify the possession on the part of individual scientists and scholars of expert knowledge. Now I take it that most people would concede the influence in all this of some elements of extraneousness and contingency, if only because we know in a general way that nothing in this world is exempt from accident. Nevertheless, I do not think it can be doubted that the academic division of labour is almost universally assumed to rest upon something far more fundamental than provisional schemes of cooperation mixed with traces of fortuitousness. It is, on the contrary, assumed to rest upon, is held to be warranted by, nothing less than the way the world actually is. The internal and external structures of the academic disciplines are grounded in a sort of ontology, an account of the constituents of reality itself. This may be a philosophically explicit position (for example, some latter-day version of the programme of positivism, or a theory of ideal languages) or it may be merely a bluff piece of scientific common sense. Either way, it is a pervasive and immensely powerful idea; it is widely supposed to have an intimate connection with the very successes of the modern university, and thus attracts to itself a sort of defensive pride; and whether it is formulated naively or knowingly it is in both cases almost irresistibly pre-emptive. What is there to be studied if it is not located under one of these rubrics? How can judgement be competent if it is not the product of accredited professional training? How can discourse itself be exact and informative if it is not one of the dialects of the universal scientific language?

Much could be said of general scope about the domination of our intellectual life by these doctrines, but that must be for another occasion. The problem for liberal education, our subject today, is that it is impossible to assign it to any definite place on this particular map of reality. Indeed, unless we chose to return to the original mediaeval trivium and quadrivium (which a few slightly dotty conservatives would in fact have us do) it would be hard to locate it on any of the maps we habitually use these days. Hence, I take it, the puzzled good will or the baffled indignation or the patronizing indifference with which proposals for liberal arts programmes are so often greeted in the modern academy. What *can* they be intending to study? Who licensed them to do it? What does it lead on to? What are their substitutes for rigour and seriousness? Is it like Kenneth Clark, or, worse still, James Burke? Why don't they stick to what they know — assuming that there is anything in particular that they do know? These kinds of questions express not simply the scandalized feelings of those who see jurisdictional boundaries being crossed and the sequences and hierarchies of specialized expertness being impudently ignored; they are the bewildered response of people who have been compelled by their own theories of meaning and taxonomies of knowledge into the deepest doubt concerning the credentials of their colleagues and the intelligibility of the enterprise those colleagues are engaged in.

It is hard to withold all sympathy from this response. One of the standing problems we have with liberal education is indeed that it is not what I may call curriculum-specific : — there is *always* a question of what it requires that we should study and teach, even when we are clear and agreed (a rare enough occurence) about what it is we wish to accomplish, and the question is only a question of means. Several interesting consequences follow from the fact.

First, there is a painful disproportion, which I judge to be inherent rather than just a common but avoidable accident, between the high purposes of liberal education and the details of the educational practices in which it is usually spelled out. A number of critics (to take a topical example) have noted the difference in the scale of Allan Bloom's jeremiad in *The Closing of the American Mind* and the scale of his pedagogic prescriptions. We are to save America from Nietzschean nihilism and democratic vulgarity by reading some Great Books in the manner recommended by Leo Strauss. Yet Bloom's case is surely not unique. One feels the same bathos in Matthew Arnold's *Culture and Anarchy*, and one's students regularly mock it in Plato when they first encounter what they think of as his prissy concern with the differences between the lax Ionian and Lydian modes and the virile and invigorating Dorian mode. I suspect that there are deep reasons for this discrepancy; but that too for another day.

Secondly, and indeed consequently, there is a temptation, a temptation I believe should be consciously resisted, to deal with this problem by importing into liberal education the curricular categories we *do* understand; for example, by making it at least *inter*-disciplinary if it cannot be straightforwardly disciplinary. After all, the disciplines are a respectable and rational sort of thing even when they are taught in small quantities within untidy packages. No doubt. But this is that very assimilation of liberal education to general education which I began by rejecting, and if the argument stood then it stands now. For that matter, the record itself of successes and failures has to be consulted. Nobody doubts that high-flying economists and philosophers will have interesting things to say to each other about (for example) the Prisoner's Dilemma; but that fact will not, alas, prevent most General Introductions to Social Science from being a dog's breakfast. (I did indeed once have a sociological colleague who volunteered for Arts One but argued for *Crime and Punishment* over *The Brothers Karamazov* on the grounds that the former, though not the latter, would call upon his expertise as a criminologist. But he must have forgotten that they are both murder mysteries.)

Thirdly, because liberal education is not curriculum-specific it is, unsurprisingly, difficult to see it as having much to do with the acquisition of particular bodies of knowledge. This probably accounts, at least in part, for the fashionable view that it has no subject matter at all and is concerned essentially with the imparting of skills, like critical thinking or aesthetic responsiveness, or some such thing. It would be too much of a disgression to contend here against this view, but it is clear that we have not had much success with it even if it is not, as I believe it to be, rooted in error. I will allow myself to say that I think it is to be found in the same contemporary desert of the mind in which we also find "values clarification" sitting where morality used to be.

What we are talking about, therefore, is a kind of empty space which we seek to fill (if we are disposed to bother at all) out of the stock of curricular categories which direct the great and distinguished mainstream of university life; or, as second resort, some of the undistinguished side streams of modern university life. But it cannot be filled in this manner, for it is a different kind of undertaking. This makes liberal education not just special but *anomalous*, and one is tempted to say that in our times it carries a perpetual burden of cognitive dissonance, for it does not conform to the terms in which we (no doubt rightly) measure the great achievements of the age.

Yet what if we were to come at the problems of liberal education upon a different set of assumptions, viewing it not in the deforming perspectives of what it pleased Clark Kerr to call "the multiversity" but in the terms described (to invoke a virtually self-recommending Canadian authority) by such as Northrop Frye? I mean, speaking all too cryptically, what if we conceive liberal education as the business of renewing the great iconic resources of the culture, in generational recurrence and at the highest feasible level of reflectiveness? This conception, to be sure, entails a complete break with the hegemonic vision of the modern university, but it can still call upon its own traditions and practices, and there is still, for a while, a saving remnant who will understand it. Would the theoretical difficulties I have been speaking about simply cease to apply, being now seen as a species of category mistake? If we succeeded in winning formal educational space for whatever gives significance to the distinctions between tradition and discovery, or wisdom and knowledge, should we then have not only a licence to attempt our task but also a compelling sense that it ought to be attempted? As Owen Barfield once said, the first question for every prisoner is whether it would be worth escaping. How *do* our fellow inmates feel about this question?

Doubtful, at best. For the truth of the matter is this. In getting our colleagues to see that liberal education is not part of the great cognitive colonization of the world which is our epoch's chief boast, we must simultaneously ask them to see that it is something else; but that something else is itself an object of scepticism or even of contempt. If one may say, following an ancient understanding, that liberal education is the most self-conscious of the ways in which we endlessly create our civilization, then one must also say that it finds its justification in the acknowledged credibility of the very claims of that civilization. Yet that is precisely what is no longer acknowledged. There are a hundred reasons for this fact, and of this hundred I have time to be telegraphically brief about no more than three or four. But they at least must be mentioned, if only to indicate the direction in which further inquiries would take us on more ample occasions.

In the first place we have to deal with a kind of cultural despair, a variety of glosses on Yeats's "The Second Coming," the sense that our times have become so incoherent that there is no set of paradigms and principles by which to organize experience or regulate conduct. One may find versions of this despair in Henry Adams and T.S. Eliot, in Ortega y Gasset and Thomas Hardy, and for that matter something not entirely unlike it is to be found at the very roots of modern sociology, from Comte to Karl Mannheim. The moral suffering behind this view makes it anything but despicable, and nobody could say that we have evidence capable of showing its falsity. It may, quite straightforwardly, be a true account of how it is with us. The trouble with such a view, of course, is that it has the character of a self-fulfilling prophesy. Believe it faithfully and it will reward your faith as we are told that faith is rewarded. So until we all find ourselves talking like Beckett's Lucky we must act as if we were facing a threat rather than submitting to a doom. But we must all be troubled by the amount of weight we have to put on the phrase "as if."

Secondly, we have a problem which I will characterize as the problem of treating education with a usuable ingenuousness and innocence of purpose. We are surrounded by fashionably reductive interpretations of education in which it is depicted as no more than part of the ideological apparatus of an oppressive state, or as an instrument for the reproduction of exploitative class relations, or as a drear rehearsal of the disciplines of the factory floor. Liberal education for its part becomes an emblem of honorific uselessness for the leisure classes, or a device for lending a fraudulent traditional authority to the cruelties of history (remember Stanford!) or an attempt to obstruct the enlightening march of modern science. There is a tincture of truth in these views, and in the right doses they are therapeutic. But like Marxist accounts of the criminal justice system, they are theories of education *suborned* rather than of education as such, and thus are ways of looking through mere appearance towards nothing whatsoever. On the whole (and I speak as one whose profession has had a large part in this) the tone has been sophomoric and the effects have been demoralizing.

Thirdly, we have to reckon with a kind of gee-whiz Marshall Macluhanite, Alvin Tofflerish, Arthur Clarkean vision of our historical situation which, given the pace of technical change and the explosion of scientific knowledge, finds all precedents obsolete, which judges the future to be completely open-ended, and which enjoins us to educate for uncertainty and the skills of adaptation. Sometimes this is tied to a view of the university itself (typified in Harold Wilson's talk about transforming Britain in the white hot crucible of technology) as the chief instrument for propelling the economy into the post-industrial era. But whether the aim be to ensure that every country has its own silicon valley or merely to help us avoid being crushed by novelty, the vision in both cases entails a judgement upon liberal education as something quaintly for another time. There is (ironically, I may add) a Baconian inheritance in all this which makes it in some ways an oddly traditional view of the world. But the truly important thing about it is that it is simultaneously excitable and provincial, and thus works with flimsy standards. It is the sort of view which (and I have heard this sais quite recently) would pronouce Philip Glass an original composer and Joseph Haydn an unoriginal composer. And as the Duke of Wellington said, if you can believe that you can believe anything.

Lastly, under this aspect of things, I will say something (certainly too little, but I fear also too much) about the idol of multiculturalism. What we understand by the term these days cannot be put in a few words, for it is a many-sided and deeply muddled theory. It is not just an untroubled recognition that complex modern societies cannot be expected to be morally homogeneous, and that on the whole it is a good thing that they can't. Nor is it, in addition, a sort of Whitmanesque celebration of an exhuberant variety of human types. Again, it goes beyond the hospitable principle that immigrants to the newer lands should not have to pay the heavy price of renouncing every element of their native culture as a condition either of citizenship or of admission to the informal spheres of social life. It is, I suppose, a failure to see the ultimate unbreakability of the connection between politics and culture, even when we have put tribalism as such far behind us. I am not just speaking about the sheer silliness of polygamy being illegal for all but Mormons, marijuana a proscribed drug for all but Rastafarians, or humane animal slaughter a requirement for all but the members of certain Islamic sects. I am speaking about the connection between civic life and personal virtue, and I am speaking about participation in the public tribunal and mastery of its particular of discourse; doing so on the assumption that such matters can never by merely *procedurally* obligatory but *substantively* indifferent and optional. And in speaking about those things I am inevitably speaking also about the education of the free intelligence and the training of the self-dependent character which such memberships and disciplines imperatively call for. Yet speaking in that fashion nowadays regularly provokes the charge, or elicits the suggestion, that one wants to restore something like Calvin's Geneva or extend something like Botha's South Africa. "Regularly" rather than "infallibly" for I have noticed that there are a few privileged exceptions, like sex role stereotyping and (guess what) inadequate levels of enthusiasm for multi culturalism. Perhaps, after all, I *have* dealt with the case of "'Shut up!' he explained."

In concentrating so heavily on the theoretical impediments to liberal education I should not want to leave the impression (if anyone were so naive as to receive it) that there are no practical difficulties. They are numerous, varied and serious, and nobody who proposes to institute or hopes to maintain a programme of liberal education can dare to ignore or hope to escape them. They take in a great deal that affects all parts of the university, but much too that falls with peculiar heaviness on this kind of educational venture. I will mention a few of them.

We have all suffered from fiscal restraint in recent years, and shall no doubt suffer from it again in future years. But that universal condition conceals the odd fact that it is the *cheap* programmes (especially if all software and no hardware) which get cut first. As C. Northcote Parkinson observed, budget committees get rid of bicycle sheds, and keep cyclotrons partly because they know what a cyclotron ought to cost but think they know good value in a bicycle shed, and partly because getting rid of the bicycle shed looks businesslike but offends no major interests. Furthermore, liberal education programmes are peripheral activities in the modern university virtually by definition, and are thus *categorically* set up for elimination or truncation in financially hard times. And then again there are the unspoken, taken-for-granted canons of what counts as expensive. Strong faculty-student ratios in graduate school are seen as nothing more than what the job requires; rations half so good in the freshman year are seen as a luxury bordering on absurdity.

Again, everybody knows, whatever may piously be said to the contrary, that publication far outweighs teaching in the scales of academic merit; but not everybody has the task of trying to recruit faculty to a programme which, for all practical purposes, neither requires nor allows anything but teaching — and for taking part in which the faculty are rewarded in predictable measure. Details will vary from one institution to another and from one department to another (one of the science departments at UBC demands fourteen papers a year for the award of tenure, one of the social science departments a mere six a year for a merit increase) but the general drift of things should be evident to anyone but Candide before he began his travels.

Analogies between the modern university and modern industry go back at least as far as Thorstein Veblen, and no doubt most of us have felt the parallel as more than a mere conceit. But the lockstep schedules, the criteria or productive efficiency, and the faceless physical environments of the modern university (indistinguishable in their monthly appearances on the cover of *University Affairs!*) are particularly and harrassingly hostile to an educational undertaking which aims at reflection and lives by conversation. It was a major cultural event at my university when someone (neither I nor David Riesman knows who) decided that the lunch hour should be treated impartially with all the other hours of the day in the scheduling of lectures. I had heard William Empson talk about the Ancient Mariner during a lunch hour, I had heard the Julliard Quartet doing Beethoven's Op. 59, No. 2, I had heard Aaron Copland speaking about his own music, and Noam Chomsky denouncing somebody or other. All this was part of my continuing liberal education — *as was the very idea of the university implicit in such possibilities!* What is one to say about the barbarism of this decision? I must hope that for the here and now it is enough to call it by its proper name.

Perhaps there are professors of chemical engineering who lose sleep over the fact that the student film society is showing *Beverly Hills Cop Two* rather that *The Battleship Potemkin*, as well as the fact that the university bookstore stocks *People Magazine* but not the *TLS*. What is certain is that those who teach the liberal studies should indeed be exercised by such facts, when facts they be. The general state of the student culture and the campus's stock of resources for those activities of the mind which don't actually earn credit are questions of central concern for our purposes. Nothing summary can be said about them here, and when one remembers Alan Bennett's description of the University of London as a device for the destruction of Bloomsbury one hesitates to put the responsibility into the hands of any kind of planner. Once again, however, the least the question deserves of us is that it be mentioned.

There is one further matter I must raise which as a peculiar and strongly consequential application to the Canadian scene. Whatever the reasons, and notwithstanding our distinctive academic excellences in this country, the fact remains that we have nothing which could stand as the equivalent of Oberlin and Antioch, Reed and Pomona, Sarah Lawrence and Dartmouth, and the hundred others we could dare to mention in the same breath. I mean that we do not have a body of colleges, like these illustratious American examples, whose special and traditional function it has been to act as centres of liberal education, so that their mere institutional continuance has kept alive both the dignity of the idea and the vitality of the practice. This means that if liberal education is to flourish in this country it must be given a place within our universities and community colleges, for we cannot hope in these times that benefactors will be found to establish Canadian Oberlins and Reeds. It will not do to predicate the Canadian university's mission (I use the cant word with misgiving) solely on the theology of the specialized graduate department and professional school, leaving the business of liberal education to an institutional sector which simply does not exist. If the thing is to be done at all it will have to be done in a place where they don't especially want it to be done. I can think of no solutions to that problem. "They" have the power of life and death over "us," but it's hard to say what can do either to or for "them." Nothing, on the other hand, is to be gained by talking as if the problem wasn't there.

Still, as Robert Merton said (rather scholastically), if a thing exists it is possible. UBC's Arts One has existed for twenty-one years, for some it has undoubtedly been possible and actual. And indeed, I hope this conference will encourage others to try what they may have thought too daunting beforehand. I will not invite anybody to believe that it is an easy undertaking, or that it is not, in Alasdair MacIntyre's phrase, thoroughly against the current of the age. But, like Jane Austen's Emma, most of us have been meaning to read more since we were fourteen years of age, and if nothing else, Arts One has at least provided an opportunity to do that while still being paid. And surely no right thinking person would be afraid of *that* prospect?

Claude Hamel

LES ORIENTATIONS
DU PREMIER CYCLE
À
L'UNIVERSITÉ DU QUÉBEC*

Je voudrais d'abord remercier les membres du Comité organisateur de m'avoir invité à prendre la parole dans le cadre de ce colloque sur le curriculum de premier cycle. J'essaierai, dans cet exposé, de faire le point sur l'état des réflexions en cours à l'Université du Québec sur les orientations du premier cycle, en situant les origines jusqu'au Colloque sur les orientations de ce cycle que nous avons tenu au Mont Ste-Anne en novembre dernier et qui rassemblait près de trois cents responsables académiques provenant de huit établissements de l'Université du Québec. Enfin, je fais état de nos réflexions actuelles à l'égard du premier cycle.

Avant de commencer, je dirai que je ne suis pas sûr d'avoir l'intention de répondre à la question, quelque peu provocatrice, retenue comme thème de ce colloque : *"Qui a peur de la formation générale?"*

Vous admettrez cependant avec moi que cette question peut être dérangeante pour une université dont les programmes professionnels doivent rencontrer les standards des organismes d'accréditation, ou qui est tentée de voir dans le succès de ses finissants aux examens d'entrée des diverses corporations une évaluation de ses performances. Elle peut être encore davantage dérangeante si l'on tient compte des

---

*La communication a été prononcée par M. Jacques Bachand, Université du Québec.

québécoises : la moitié des étudiants de premier cycle sont inscrits à un certificat; plus de la moitié des étudiants de premier cycle suivent caractéristiques générales de la population étudiante des universités leurs études à temps partiel, le tiers sont âgés de trente ans ou plus.

C'est à cause de ces caractéristiques fondamentales que je sens le besoin d'effectuer un bref retour en arrière sur les origines de l'Université du Québec, d'où émanent, en partie, les préoccupations actuelles sur les orientations des études de premier cycle.

1. ORIGINES DES PRÉOCCUPATIONS

L'Université du Québec célèbre, cette année, son vingtième anniversaire. Créée en décembre 1968, par une loi de l'Assemblée nationale, l'Université du Québec recevait ses premiers étudiants en septembre 1969. Ce *réseau d'institutions publiques* implantées dans la plupart des régions du Québec recevait comme missions, outre de développer l'enseignement et la recherche, de favoriser l'accès aux études universitaires, particulièrement pour ce qui est des personnes qui en sont traditionnellement éloignées pour des raisons géographiques ou sociologiques et, de façon plus spécifique, de contribuer à la formation des enseignants.

L'Université du Québec et ses constituantes se voyaient également confier le mandat de contribuer au développement économique, social et culturel des régions du Québec, en fonction des besoins et des ressources de celles-ci.

Profitant de sa création pour ainsi dire spontanée, l'Université du Québec s'est dotée de formules pédagogiques et intellectuelles novatrices en milieu universitaire, qui semblaient mieux correspondre à ses missions.

Rejetant le modèle facultaire, l'on choisit de rattacher les programmes à une structure autonome distincte des départements : *les modules*. Chaque module est géré par un conseil où siègent des professeurs appartenant à divers départements et oeuvrant dans le programme, des étudiants et des représentants du milieu socio-économique concerné.

Dégagés de l'emprise des départements, les programmes pouvaient s'ouvrir à toutes les disciplines et suivre l'évolution des besoins du milieu. Cette formule avait en outre l'avantage de permettre une utilisation maximale des cours offerts par les départements.

Les règlements pédagogiques qui furent élaborés étaient eux aussi marqués du signe de l'innovation. L'Université avait choisi de définir son enseignement par l'éducation permanente et son régime des études le reflétait: tous les étudiants inscrits à un programme étaient considérés comme des étudiants réguliers, qu'il s'agisse de "jeunes" en processus de formation continue et inscrits à temps plein ou "d'adultes" effectuant un retour aux études après plusieurs années d'absence du système scolaire et inscrits à temps partiel. Tous les programmes étaient accessibles aux adultes qui, n'ayant pas de diplôme d'études collégiales ou un diplôme équivalent, possédaient les connaissances appropriées et une expérience jugée pertinente. Une politique de reconnaissance des acquis était en outre instaurée suivant le principe qu'il faut éviter la reprise de cours conduisant à une formation ou à des connaissances déjà acquises. Une formule de programme court de 30 crédits adaptée aux besoins des adultes, les certificats, fut aussi mis au point.

Dans la poursuite de sa mission d'assurer l'accessibilité aux études universitaires, notamment sur le plan géographique, chaque université constituante se dota d'un réseau de centres d'enseignement hors-campus. Le réseau créa un établissement voué à l'enseignement à distance : la Télé-Université.

Contraintes de planifier leur développement dans un contexte de ressources financières limitées, les unités constituantes de l'Université du Québec se dotèrent d'axes de développement académique complémentaires les uns par rapport aux autres et en conformité avec les besoins de leur région d'insertion. C'est autour de ces champs d'excellence que devait se bâtir la programmation offerte dans les établissements, du bacalauréat au doctorat.

Parallèlement à toutes ces préoccupations, l'Université du Québec jugea nécessaire de se donner, dès ses premières années, une philosophie et des objectifs généraux qui devaient orienter les études de premier cycle. Adopté en avril 1974, cet énoncé de principes devait inspirer tout projet de nouveau programme.

L'énoncé de la philosophie et des objectifs généraux du premier cycle cherchait à préciser *les finalités du premier cycle* en le décrivant en fonction, d'une part, de l'ordre d'enseignement qui le précède, le niveau collégial, et, d'autre part, des études supérieures ou de l'exercice d'une profession. Ces finalités s'exprimaient comme suit : du point de vue scientifique, porter une attention particulière à la méthodologie et aux fondements aussi bien théoriques qu'empiriques de la discipline ou du champ d'études, et assurer ainsi les assises nécessaires pour suivre l'évolution des connaissances; du point de vue de l'apprentissage, viser par des activités pédagogiques appropriées à l'affirmation des qualités suivantes :

- au plan intellectuel, rendre l'étudiant assez autonome pour poursuivre ses études, assez polyvalent pour relier sa problématique à celle d'autres spécialités et suffisamment critique pour analyser scientifiquement les situations sociales, les argumentations et les idéologies;
- au plan volitif, permettre à l'étudiant d'identifier des attitudes d'ordre éthique pour l'exercice de la profession, pour la pratique de la science et pour la conduite de la vie; d'ordre esthétique pour les capacités culturelles;
- au plan social, rendre l'étudiant capable de comprendre l'évolution de la société et d'y intervenir efficacement par sa compétence professionnelle ou scientifique.

C'est par la spécialisation dans une discipline ou un champ d'études que ces finalités devaient être atteintes. Il ne s'agissait cependant pas de la spécialisation pour elle-même, telle qu'elle est recherchée aux études avancées, mais plutôt d'assurer les assises d'une connaissance objective, structurée, rigoureuse. L'examen des fondements aussi bien théoriques qu'empiriques de la discipline ou du champ d'étude devait caractériser un bon nombre d'activités pédagogiques du programme et constituer une initiation véritable à une méthodologie disciplinaire tout en assurant un solide corpus de connaissances. Le reste des activités du programme devait être davantage orienté vers l'acquisition de connaissances particulières ou vers la maîtrise des techniques propres à l'exercice d'une profession conforme à ce niveau d'études.

Traduites en *objectifs généraux*, ces finalités s'exprimaient de la façon suivante :

Au terme de son premier cycle universitaire, l'étudiant devrait avoir suffisamment développé, dans et par sa discipline ou son champ d'études, les qualités suivantes :
- l'autonomie, c'est-à-dire la capacité de diriger lui-même sa démarche intellectuelle et de suivre l'évolution ultérieure des connaissances dans sa discipline, son champ d'études ou sa profession;
- la communication, c'est-à-dire la capacité de rendre accessibles les ressources et les instruments de sa discipline ou de son champ d'études et la capacité de profiter des ressources et des instruments de disciplines ou de champs d'études connexes au sien;
- l'esprit critique, c'est-à-dire la capacité d'analyser scientifiquement les argumentations et les idéologies, et la capacité de faire une lecture critique des situations sociales, culturelles et politiques de son milieu de vie;
- la créativité, c'est-à-dire la capacité de donner d'autres dimensions à son objet d'études en lui associant de nouveaux éléments et en questionnant ses finalités, et la capacité de participer à la transformation de la société et au renouvellement des valeurs;
- la mobilité, c'est-à-dire la capacité de s'adapter aux situations changeantes de la société et aux pratiques nouvelles de sa profession;
- le service à la communauté, c'est-à-dire la capacité de traduire constamment sa formation et ses connaissances en une contribution sociale valable, compte tenu des divers besoins de son milieu de vie.

2. CHANGEMENTS DE CONJONCTURE

Le rapide survol que je viens d'effectuer couvre en fait les dix premières années d'existence du réseau de l'Université du Québec. Durant cette période, il faut admettre qu'une bonne part des énergies déployées dans le réseau furent monopolisées par son développement physique. Celui-ci fut marqué par l'implantation de nouvelles constituantes, l'installation des campus, une croissance phénoménale des effectifs étudiants, le recrutement des professeurs, la multiplication des nouveaux programmes et des options à l'intérieur des programmes existants. Simultanément, les universités québécoises étaient aux prises avec des difficultés financières importantes liées au sous-financement, par le gouvernement, des nouveaux effectifs étudiants. Une série de facteurs internes et externes à l'Université du Québec allaient amener un changement dans ses préoccupations.

2.1 Facteurs internes

Dès le début des années 1980, les doyens des études de premier cycle des constituantes du réseau (il n'y a pas de faculté à l'Université du Québec, et le doyen du premier cycle est responsable de l'ensemble des enseignements de ce cycle) entre- prirent une réflexion importante sur les objectifs généraux du premier cycle. Celle-ci émanait d'une question fort simple : "Comment mesurer l'atteinte des objectifs du premier cycle par les étudiants?" L'on se rendit compte que ces objec- tifs n'avaient pas prise sur la formation des étudiants. L'on n'en tenait à peu près pas compte dans l'évaluation des programmes et pas du tout dans celle des étudiants.

La maîtrise de la langue en constitue une belle illustration. L'exis- tence d'un objectif général relié aux capacités de communiquer n'a pas empêché que des étudiants ne possédant pas une maîtrise convenable du français puissent obtenir un diplôme universitaire.

D'autres facteurs nous ont amenés à nous demander si les objectifs fixés en 1974 étaient toujours valables.

En douze ans, l'Université du Québec a beaucoup changé. Comme dans les autres universités québécoises, le tiers des étudiants sont inscrits en sciences de l'administration.

Les programmes de certificats se sont multipliés et sont aujourd'hui presque aussi nombreux que les programmes de grade.

Des études effectuées sur la persévérance des étudiants et le taux de diplomation ont montré que les abandons étaient très nombreux. Sans doute comme dans les autres universités; néanmoins la situation est préoccupante.

La proportion de chargés de cours par rapport aux professeurs régu- liers n'a cessé de croître. Les chargés de cours comptent aujourd'hui pour la moitié des ressources professorales totales des universités qué- bécoises.

Enfin, l'on constate un désintéressement de plus en plus marqué des professeurs réguliers vis-à-vis de l'enseignement au premier cycle, ceux-ci préférant se consacrer aux études avancées et à la recherche.

2.2 Facteurs externes

Je n'ai pas le temps de m'attarder sur les multiples facteurs externes qui, à tout le moins depuis le début des années 1980, nous ont amenés à nous interroger sur la formation de premier cycle. Il y eut bien sûr la récession économique et ses impacts terribles sur le chômage des jeunes,

y compris les diplômés universitaires. Il y a eut les changements struc
turels du marché de l'emploi. Un grand nombre d'études et de rapports
produits par le ministère de l'Enseignement supérieur et de la Science,
le Conseil des universités, le Conseil supérieur de l'éducation, des
commissions d'études *ad hoc* sur les universités au Québec, l'éducation des adultes, etc., remettaient en cause la formation de premier
cycle. Certaines universités québécoises avaient aussi entrepris leurs
propres réflexions. Il y avait enfin tout le mouvement américain de
réforme du premier cycle universitaire amorcé dès le milieu des années
1970 et où bon nombre d'universitaires québécois croyaient avoir trouvé
un modèle à suivre.

Il faut savoir qu'au Québec, on ne passe pas directement du secondaire
à l'université, après onze années d'école. On entre à l'université
après deux ans de collège, qui est un ordre autonome d'enseignement.

3. COLLOQUE DU MONT STE-ANNE

C'est dans ce contexte que l'Université du Québec a organisé le Colloque
du Mont Ste-Anne, les 4 et 5 novembre 1987. Cet événement se voulait la
première étape d'une réflexion collective de l'Université du Québec sur
les orientations du premier cycle. Il s'adressait en premier lieu aux
professeurs du réseau exerçant des responsabilités de gestion académique
et visait entre autres objectifs : à les sensibiliser aux questions de
la formation de premier cycle; à diagnostiquer l'état du premier cycle
et à évaluer les besoins de réforme dans le réseau de l'Université du
Québec; à renforcer la cohésion du réseau de l'Université du Québec en
matière de philosophie de programmes et d'objectifs de formation; à
amorcer, s'il y a lieu, les réflexions sur la reformulation éventuelle
des objectifs du premier cycle.

Cette réflexion, qui dépassait le seul cadre des programmes, devait
s'attacher à couvrir le premier cycle dans sa globalité, c'est-à-dire
également son amont, le niveau collégial, et son aval, les études
avancées et le marché du travail.

Sept thèmes de discussion leur étaient proposés :
- la philosophie et les objectifs du premier cycle : bilan et
  prospective;
- la formation;
- l'éducation permanente;
- le marché du travail;
- la pédagogie;
- l'évaluation;
- les études avancées.

Je vais maintenant vous livrer les principales préoccupations qui se
sont dégagées des discussions.

Le colloque a montré que les objectifs généraux du premier cycle,
proposés en 1974, paraissaient toujours pertinents bien qu'ils soient

tombés quelque peu dans l'oubli depuis. Les programmes semblent se définir essentiellement à partir de leurs objectifs spécifiques.

Les objectifs généraux ont toutefois été jugés de formulation trop générale, difficilement opérationnels au plan des programmes et des cours et difficilement vérifiables en termes d'atteinte par les étudiants.

Par rapport à ce souci d'opérationalisation, l'on s'est demandé s'il n'était pas utopique de chercher à définir des objectifs généraux uniques pour tous les genres de programmes, tant les certificats que les baccalauréats, et pour toutes les disciplines et tous les champs d'études.

Parmi les six autres thèmes de réflexion proposés, deux ont plus particulièrement retenu l'attention des participants : la formation et la pédagogie. Cette faveur montre certainement l'intérêt que les professeurs portent à ces questions fondamentales.

En ce qui concerne la formation, c'est l'articulation ou plutôt l'absence d'articulation entre les niveaux collégial et universitaire qui semble constituer l'obstacle majeur à l'atteinte de la qualité. La spécialisation du premier cycle universitaire ne peut avoir de sens que si elle s'appuie sur une solide formation générale qui devrait être acquise au cegep. Un meilleur arrimage entre les deux ordres d'enseignement apparaît aujourd'hui absolument nécessaire, tout le monde le reconnaît. Il faut maintenant trouver le moyen d'y arriver.

Les exigences des corporations professionnelles ont été identifiées comme l'une des causes de la surspécialisation des programmes universitaires. Comment peut-on s'en démarquer? Comment y arriver sans une concertation entre les différentes universités?

Les programmes de premier cycle eux-mêmes semblent souvent orientés vers l'information plus que vers la formation. Si elles sont des ensembles cohérents, les unités de cours apparaissent parfois assez discontinues, indépendantes les unes des autres. Il faudrait faire en sorte que les professeurs soient davantage au fait du rôle et de la place qu'occupent les cours dans le programme et donc de la raison de leur enseignement dans la formation des étudiants. Une telle démarche contribuerait à assurer la formation fondamentale recherchée au premier cycle.

Le Colloque a aussi montré que la pédagogie constituait une préoccupation marquée des professeurs. S'ils semblent se désintéresser du premier cycle, c'est peut-être parce que l'enseignement n'est pas valorisé à l'Université, comme l'est la recherche. La capacité d'enseigner ne devrait-elle pas être considérée lors de l'évaluation des professeurs ou lors de leur promotion? Ne devrait-elle pas constituer un critère d'embauche au même titre que la capacité de faire de la recherche?

Les discussions intervenues sur les autres thèmes du Colloque ont aussi permis de confirmer que l'Université du Québec devrait maintenir son ouverture vis-à-vis des adultes et leur intégration à la clintèle régulière de l'Université. Si la formule des certificats paraît adaptée à leurs besoins et à leurs conditions de vie, l'existence de ces programmes ne devrait pas avoir pour effet de détourner les jeunes des programmes de grade.

Par ailleurs, les taux élevés d'abandon constatés chez les adultes constituent un phénomène préoccupant qu'il importe d'examiner de près.

C'est dans le même contexte que l'Université devrait revoir ses pratiques en matière d'évaluation. S'il se fait beaucoup d'évaluations à l'Université du Québec, évaluations des programmes, des étudiants, des enseignements, des professeurs, l'on ne s'est pas vraiment interrogé sur les objectifs que ces évaluations devraient poursuivre et sur les liens qui devraient exister entre toutes ces formes d'évaluation.

L'évaluation devrait constituer l'instrument privilégié de toute réorientation des études de premier cycle.

Les discussions entourant les points de sortie du premier cycle, les études avancées et le marché du travail, ont permis de mettre en évidence des problèmes importants qui devront être étudiés en profondeur. Quant aux liens que l'Université doit maintenir avec le marché du travail, ils doivent lui laisser suffisamment de marge de manoeuvre pour lui permettre d'être à l'écoute des attentes des entreprises sans en être à la remorque ou s'y coller servilement. L'Université aurait avantage à profiter plus de la présence des membres socio-économiques sur les conseils de module pour renforcer ces liens.

Plusieurs professeurs ont déploré l'existence d'une coupure nette entre le premier cycle et le deuxième cycle, qui serait même plus grande à certains égards que celle séparant le premier cycle du collégial.

Cette coupure se traduirait par le faible taux de passage du baccalauréat à la maîtrise. Parmi les facteurs évoqués pour expliquer ce faible taux de passage, l'on a évoqué: la trop grande spécialisation des programmes disciplinaires de premier cycle, qui ne fournissent pas une préparation adéquate pour entreprendre des études supérieures et ne suscitent pas suffisamment la curiosité des étudiants pour leur donner le goût de faire de la recherche; le peu d'implication des professeurs actifs en recherche dans l'enseignement au premier cycle; la problématique de la situation économique de l'étudiant gradué de même que la rareté des débouchés dans plusieurs secteurs pour les diplômés du deuxième cycle; l'insuffisance de l'encadrement des étudiants du premier cycle, lequel pourrait stimuler leur intérêt pour la recherche.

4. CONCLUSION

Comme vous pouvez le constater, le Colloque du Mont Ste-Anne a suscité beaucoup plus de questions qu'il n'a apporté de réponses. C'était d'ailleurs là le but recherché : enclencher un mouvement de réflexion sur le premier cycle considéré dans sa globalité, en n'évitant aucune remise en question et en ne prenant rien pour acquis.

Amorcées collectivement, les réflexions se poursuivent maintenant dans chacune des unités constituantes, où les débats impliquent cette fois l'ensemble du corps professoral, de même que les étudiants. Pour éviter la dispersion et profiter au maximum de ces réflexions, nous prévoyons tenir au cours de l'année 1988-1989 trois mini-colloques qui constitueront des moments d'échanges et de mises en commun autour des questions fondamentales dégagées jusqu'à maintenant, dont, notamment, les suivantes : Comment rendre les objectifs du premier cycle opérationnels vis-à-vis des programmes et de la formation? Faut-il les reformuler, les adapter, les modifier? Sont-ils applicables à la fois aux certificats et aux baccalauréats, aux étudiants à temps partiel? Comment en faire des paramètres d'évaluation?

Cette réflexion sur les orientations du premier cycle à l'Université du Québec devra avoir une portée systémique, c'est-à-dire rejoindre les préoccupations reliées à cet ordre d'enseignement de l'ensemble du réseau, quelles que soient la taille des unités constituantes et leur situation institutionnelle respective, même si, en pratique, la question de la spécialisation des programmes se pose différemment selon la taille de l'établissement. C'est ainsi qu'il faudra s'assurer que les mesures qui seront prises pour améliorer la qualité de la formation se répercutent jusque dans les centres d'enseignement hors-campus et rejoignent les étudiants à temps partiel.

Elle devrait permettre également de compléter l'éventail des programmes offerts dans ses établissements qui souffrent encore de lacunes importantes dans les secteurs disciplinaires de base. Séquelles de la logique du développement planifié selon des axes prédéterminés ou conséquences de la petite taille des unités constituantes des régions périphériques, ce besoin de nouveaux programmes pourra sans doute être plus facilement comblé en privilégiant une approche plus fondamentale ou plus générale de la formation, en tous cas certainement moins spécialisée qu'elle ne l'est présentement, compte tenu de ce que coûte cette spécialisation.

Pour être considérée comme une réussite, cette réflexion sur les orientations du premier cycle devra concourir à la réalisation des missions pour lesquelles le Québec a voulu se doter d'une université publique. Comme toutes les autres institutions d'enseignement supérieur, l'Université du Québec doit viser l'excellence, mais celle-ci ne saurait se mesurer autrement que par l'atteinte de l'idéal pour lequel elle a été créée.

Peter Morgan

ASPIRATION TOWARDS THE
UNITY OF KNOWLEDGE
AT TORONTO

> I want to try to tie the
> whole thing together,
> Helen Caldicott*

This is a rather hubristic title, since I sometimes doubt whether more than one person at the University of Toronto is interested in the notion of the Unity of Knowledge. However, I believe that it is an important notion, both intellectually and socially. I can cite recent authorities in support of it. Hans-Georg Gadamer says : "One has to make distinctions, to be sure, but even more one has to see things in their inter-relations" (quoted by Jürgen Habermas, *Philosophical-Political Profiles*, tr. Lawrence, 1985, 192). Ervin Laszlo says :

> I am looking for harmony. To me that which makes the most sense, that which is most real, is that which is the most general. This immediately puts me at odds with most specialists and the majority of the contemporary scientific establishment. (*Zygon*, June 1988, 177)

He continues :

> Eventually we might work our way toward an integrated understanding of all that there is in the general stream of experience. We will not do this in every detail. (178)

---

*Peace Magazine, June/July 1988, 17.

Also Alfred Kazin has recently written :

> I am sympathetic to (the) essentially religious belief that there is a
> fundamental unity to nature that must be recognized and realized in
> the human soul. It would seem to me that all the leading physicists
> must believe in that unity and that their researches prove it. But,
> alas, not all scientists and intellectuals favor such an favor such an
> ancient idealism. (*New York Times Book Review*, 1 May 1988, 41)

It is important to go back to the notion of the Unity of Knowledge in
reaction against the excessive specialization which has led to the
conflict of cultures which C.P. Snow identified decades ago. In my
opinion, over-specialization is fundamentally damaging because it has
led to a separation in leading intellectual milieux, stemming from the
universities. A crucial by-product of this separation has been over-
funded scientific specialization which has led all too easily to technological application in the field of nuclear weaponry. We have to draw
back from the abyss which this has produced. This withdrawal takes the
form not only of a rational decision to cut back the number of weapons,
as is presently being attempted by statesmen, but also of a general
reappraisal of the steps, including specialization and a perversion of
the educational system, which has led to it. My hope is that the
programme which I will go on to outline in this presentation may prove
to be a modest step in this direction. At least just about all I can do
as an academic in order to help achieve the overriding goal of a just
peace is to work towards the implementation of the programme. It is
noteworthy that scientists themselves are most concerned about
improving the way things are done. This is evident amongst those
involved in developing the present programme, as well as those active
in "Science for Peace." Of course the problem is not restricted to
one particular field, however salient that is. Ivan Head comments :

> one out of every four scientists and technologists in the entire world
> engaged in research and development is working on weapons. Not on
> nutrition, not on AIDS, not on education, but weapons. (*Globe and
> Mail*, 20 July 1987, A7)

The problem in my view is that of the general mind-set that leads to
this slanting of attention.

"Unity of Knowledge" was the original name of a programme developed
at University College, University of Toronto, now called the Integrated
Studies Programme, because "Unity of Knowledge" is too bold. The
programme, which I will here outline, comprises three segments entitled
"Expression," "Behaviour" and "Science," with "Analysis" and "Multiple
Aspects." The first three stand for the established division into
Humanities, Human Sciences, and Natural Sciences. "Analysis" is added,
in order to provide the necessary mathematical tool for serious scientific work. "Expression" focuses on language, its nature, its use by

the student, and its presence in literary and philosophical texts. "Behaviour" draws on material from psychology, sociology and economics; "Science" on material from physics and biology. The method is pragmatic, based on the scholarly bents of those involved in developing the programme. The present programme was the product in the first instance of cooperation amongst an economist, a physicist and a literary historian. A different mix would have produced a different programme with different emphases within it. I myself hope that the programme will be flexible enough to allow for the input of contributors from quite different fields, for example, from the side of the social sciences, a historian, political scientist, sociologist or anthropologist; from the side of the natural sciences, a biologist; from the side of the humanities, a philosopher. Such flexibility is desirable and indeed will have to be a feature of the programme as it is implemented in the future.

The programme is thus pragmatic, based on the experience and interests of individuals teaching and researching within the ambience of the University of Toronto. We have been at least subliminally influenced by the thought and writing of our distinguished predecessors Harold Innes the economist, Marshall McLuhan the cultural critic, and Northrop Frye the literary critic. McLuhan in particular sought "to open the intercommunication between several fields"; he recognized more than we have done what he called "underlying unities of form."[1] It is noteworthy that in the last two cases the quest for general and broad understanding has deep spiritual underpinnings : McLuhan an ardent Catholic and Frye a minister of the United Church of Canada.

If one looks at the programme which has emerged (fig. 1) through the sustained effort of a large College committee, four basic principles appear to underlie it. These I will call : 1. structure, 2. synecdoche, 3. focus, 4. interaction.

1. Structurally, the programme is basically tripartite, covering the areas of the humanities, the social, and the natural sciences. However, in order to achieve a breakaway from traditional categories and departmental fiefdoms, the sections have been given the names indicated above.

2. Synecdoche means the part standing for the whole. "You can't study everything," so the small segment has to do duty for the larger field of which it is part. Thus, language in the "Expression" unit stands for human expression.

3. Focus means that the individual segment points to a single goal. The aim is for the student to achieve a competence in basic scholarly activity in the three basic areas. She will finally apply this knowledge to the study of a particular human problem in the "Multiple Aspects" segment. Thus the aim is practical and the focus specific. In the nineteenth-century conservative thought of Cardinal Newman this centre would have been provided by theology, which he considered to be the queen of the sciences. As pragmatists we lack even the philosophical centre, such as a phenomenologist like Husserl might have

suggested (see his *Crisis of European Sciences*, 1954). Instead, we have the segment called "Multiple Aspects." Here what has been learned of Expression, Behaviour, and Science will be applied in relation to a particular topic, for example a human artefact, such as the photograph, or a community, such as the Atomic Energy of Canada facility at Chalk River, Ontario. The work in this segment where what has been learned is tested and applied should be both provocative and productive.

4. Interactive has not yet been fully achieved, but it will be as the programme is taught and developed. This involves gaining a sense of the actual compatibility of the different modes of knowledge.

The programme is intended as a "minor," compatible with specialization in most particular disciplines, with the significant and regrettable exception of programmes in the hard sciences. It has been fully fleshed out at the College level. The programme is thought of as providing the general understanding needed by anyone who is to make an informed contribution to the discussion and resolution of the major social and environmental problems that will face us in the twenty-first century. It could well be and perhaps should be considered as preparation for professional training in law, medicine, business and teaching. Unfortunately, it has *not yet been implemented*. It still lacks funding and academic approval by the Faculty of Arts and Science.

The phrase Unity of Knowledge provides one way of sensing the wholeness and integrity of the programme. I cling to the phrase also partly because it is meaningful to two Egyptian colleagues, Professors Mourad Wahba and Mona Abousenna who invited me to discuss the issue and the programme in Cairo last spring. Professor Wahba has edited a valuable collection of essays by distinguished international scholars on the topic (Cairo, 1983). His own tripartite division of it is very suggestively named "Politics, Physics, Philosophy." To these I would have to add "Poetry." In Toronto we advanced in a pragmatic way, but using Wahba's terms we would have reached a different but perhaps even more challenging curriculum. Wahba has not produced our concrete course of study. His ambition rather seems to be to expose his colleagues to the notion of the Unity of Knowledge and thus trigger a mental ferment out of which a course of study will emerge.

Back in Toronto our proposed college programme may be swamped by important recent developments in the Faculty of Arts and Science. The Faculty will probably revamp its offerings as it has done over the past years after the McPherson and the Kelly reports: McPherson the distinguished political scientist and Kelly the Principal of St. Michael's College. The present Faculty committee is headed by my colleague in English Dean Eleanor Cook. The aim (indicated in a recent working report, June 1988) is to counter "over-specialization" by proposing generalized study at the beginning, crossing the boundaries amongst the Humanities, the Human Sciences and the Natural Sciences, before focusing as the student's career continues. This pattern is expressed by dramatic diagrams (figs. 2-4). The notion is for students to take courses, perhaps some of them new, from amongst the general areas, before going on to specialize in later years.

I think that this is a very desirable report. It is clearly in line with the stirrings across North America to which this conference is a witness. I would hope that our own Integrated Studies Programme still makes a helpful contribution in being already fully worked out in detail, through the novelty and fulness of its course descriptions, and most importantly by the sense of integration which it possesses. The Faculty scheme looks like a tree, or a barbed arrow pointed up to the sky : or a bunch of these. The movement is dynamically, progressively, aggressively forward chronologically in terms of the student's career in the direction of specialization (not the "over-specialization" which has been eschewed). I think that in our programme we are offering a more allusive and more organic image, not that of the target, but that of the unfolding flower. The petals of the flower radiate from its centre, but remain attached to it. Naturalistically, the flower represents a sense of intellectual and emotional balance which students surely need as leaders and as participants in a volatile, problematical and dangerous world.

For purposes of comparison, such as it was suggested that I attempt in preparing this paper, it would be necessary to gain an understanding of procedures which vary from university to university, college to college, school to school, province to province, indeed country to country, as indicated above in making a connection between Canada and Egypt, and in the consideration given at this Conference to the link between developments in Canada and the United States. I have myself made personal and tentative overtures in the direction of the Faculty of Education at my own university, the Ontario Institute of Studies in Higher Education, York University, Ryerson Polytechnical Institute and the community colleges. Professor Michael Skolnik of OISE, who will address the Conference, was sympathetic. Professor Alan Coman of the Faculty of Education also sympathized with the thrust of the programme, but his own view was more expansive. He would like to see more integration amongst disciplines. He sees the decline of subject specialization, in both the schools and the Faculty of Education, with the inevitable influence of the media. Professor Norman Feltes, Chairman of the Department of English at York University, was also sympathetic. Like Coman, he observed the decline of subject specialization. He found value in a resort to theory and was optimistic about changes on the basis of burgeoning democratic interest amongst students and colleagues.

I asked my colleague Norman Mackenzie of Ryerson Polytechnic for comments on the situation there and in the Ontario community colleges. He referred me to an able report by Anthony Wilkinson, President of Lambton College, Sarnia, entitled *Post-Secondary Education in a Changing Society*, 1986. From my own perspective I cannot help but read this as largely the work of a specialist who thinks of the role that the polytechnic can play in response to a challenge to Canadian business enterprise in the global market-place. As I have indicated above, I cannot accept his premise that meeting such a challenge has to be our first priority. Wilkinson divides the work-force to be educated between the minority comprised of highly skilled technologists and the majority, the product of what he chillingly calls "dumbing down." However, he does recognize the value of a general education both for the technological elite and the rest (especially when he writes towards the end of his report, "compartmentalised disciplines would be a hindrance") (pp. 42, 50). "The need is for transferable, intellectual skills, including an appropriate skill base rather than for restrictive vocationalism" (p. 53). "The educational system must consider the development of the flexible generalist" (p. 54). He writes of the need for "education for living" (p. 58). In this final part of his study the aims of Wilkinson for the community colleges are compatible with ours within the university. I feel that the essence of our own programme proposal is its flexibility: the content of the programme must vary according to the qualifications and interests of those teaching it, as well as the students in it. A technological component indeed could be added or infiltrated. This is particularly relevant in the focal course "Multiple Aspects" where we apply what we have learned in different areas to a particular human situation. Here a knowledgeable assessment of the technological component of the situation is of crucial importance. The programme itself, though in its present form all too academic, could be adjusted to different educational levels. It is so modest in size that it can be assimilated to a larger programme of specialized (for example, technological) study.

The developments, as indicated in our own programme related to the notion of the Unity of Knowledge, concern with this in Egypt and the United States, the responses of Professor Skolnik of OISE, Professor Coman of the Faculty of Education, University of Toronto, Professor Feltes of the Department of English, York University, with Mr Wilkinson's report on movements within the community colleges — these all clearly respond to a sense of ferment which is also to be found in the rest of the educational system of the whole country, indeed, the world, as this conference shows.

1. McLuhan, *Letters*, ed. Molinaro, McLuhan and Toye, 1987, 218, 223 (1951). Alan Coman points out to me that Frye rejects the generalist approach.

FIGURE 1. SCHEDULE OF COURSES

	Year I	Year II	Year III
Fall	Science I Analysis I Human Expression I	Analysis III Human Behaviour II	Human Behaviour III Human Expression III* Integrated Studies II*
Spring	Science II Analysis II Human Behaviour I	Human Expression II Integrated Studies I	Science III Human Expression III (cont.) Integrated Studies II (cont.)

*These are half-courses which extend through two terms.

FIGURE 2

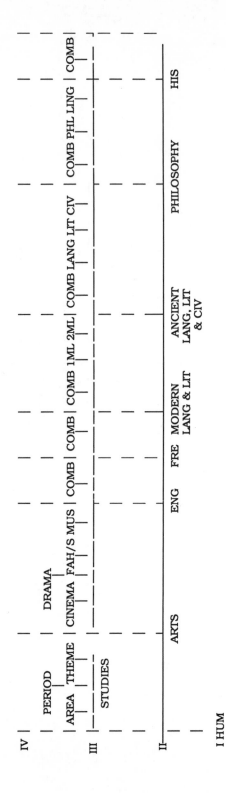

FIGURE 3

SOCIAL SCIENCES

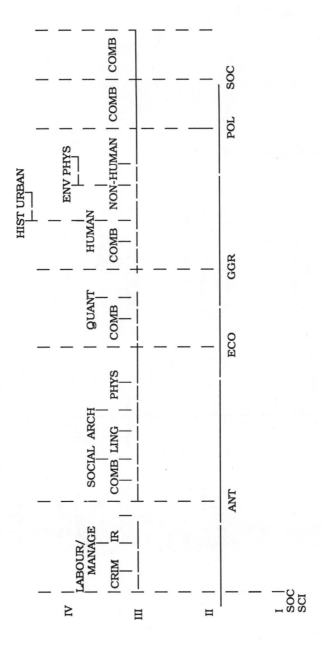

SCIENCES

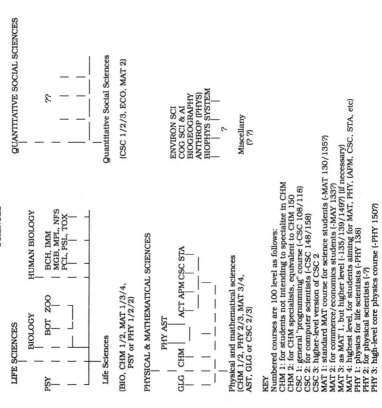

LIFE SCIENCES

BIOLOGY   HUMAN BIOLOGY

PSY   BOT ZOO   BCH, IMM / MGB, MPL, NFS / PCL, PSL, TOX

Life Sciences

(BIO, CHM 1/2, MAT 1/3/4, PSY or PHY 1/2/2)

PHYSICAL & MATHEMATICAL SCIENCES

PHY AST

GLG CHM   ACT APM CSC STA

Physical and mathematical sciences
(CHM 1/2, PHY 2/3, MAT 3/4, AST, GLG or CSC 2/3)

QUANTITATIVE SOCIAL SCIENCES

??

Quantitative Social Sciences

(CSC 1/2/3, ECO, MAT 2)

ENVIRON SCI
COG SCI & AI
BIOGEOGRAPHY
ANTHROP (PHYS)
BIOPHYS SYSTEM
?

Miscellany
(? ?)

KEY
Numbered courses are 100 level as follows:
CHM 1: for students not intending to specialize in CHM
CHM 2: for CHM specialists, equivalent to CHM 150
CSC 1: general "programming" course (-CSC 108/118)
CSC 2: for computer scientists (-CSC 148/158)
CSC 3: higher-level version of CSC 2
MAT 1: standard MAT course for science students (-MAT 130/135?)
MAT 2: for commerce/economics students (-MAY 133?)
MAT 3: as MAT 1, but higher level (-135/139/149?) (if necessary)
MAT 4: highest level, for students aiming for MAT, PHY, (APM, CSC, STA, etc)
PHY 1: physics for life scientists (-PHY 138)
PHY 2: for physical scientists (-?)
PHY 3: high-level core physics course (-PHY 150?)

Michael L. Skolnik

SOME OBSERVATIONS
ON
THE STATE OF
AND THE PROSPECTS FOR
LIBERAL EDUCATION IN
CANADIAN UNIVERSITIES

As one who tries to keep up with current issues and developments in Canadian higher education, I feel privileged to have been given the opportunity to summarize and comment on the major themes which emerged at this conference on liberal education. Before proceeding to substantive observations, a few introductory remarks of a procedural nature are in order.

My objectives in this paper are to highlight key issues, questions, and themes which emerged in the plenary sessions and workshops; to attempt to bring greater focus and order to our treatment of liberal education than the parliamentary-style discussions which we had normally facilitate; and to draw some conclusions that may be pertinent to the advancement of liberal education in Canadian universities. These objectives of synthesis and generalization necessitate some sacrifice of particulars, and in that regard I beg indulgence of participants, and especially of *rapporteurs*, for such of their excellent commentaries and summaries which my task requires that I omit from my remarks.

I think it appropriate that I incorporate some comments upon things which were not said here, in order to help flesh out a larger map within which I can place what was said. In constructing this map, I will refer to some of the higher education literature which is relevant to a fulsome discussion of the state of liberal education and potential directions for reform of that endeavor.

91

Finally, I must acknowledge that, like others who are drawn to a conference of this type, I am not an entirely neutral observer. I suspect that few of us would have spent this weekend cloistered together if we did not believe strongly in the value of liberal education and have some concerns as to whether what is being done in this realm presently is enough or is good enough. It is important, however, that in my role, I try as well as is possible to set aside my own biases and aim for an impartial treatment of the subject. Indeed, recognizing my own biases and those which I sensed of most participants, if anything I shall try to err on the side of being critical of our inherent tendencies to lapse into rhapsodic and romantic reveries about liberal education — bearing in mind Weber's ideal that the scholar should always be more skeptical of research findings that conform to his or her preconceived notions than those which do not.[2] Thus, the tenor of my comments to a group like this, of like-minded colleagues, will be different than if I were before a group of what Ortega Y Gassett described as "the new barbarians," those who value only specialized professional knowledge.[3]

WHAT'S THE PROBLEM?

The terms of reference for the conference emphasized "canvassing possibilities, analyzing obstacles, and describing cases," and discouraged expenditure of effort on discussion of the nature and definition of liberal education. The strength of this steering decision by the conference organizers is that it enabled participants to come away with some very practical information on how liberal education has been operationalized in various institutions and the obstacles that were encountered in these initiatives, rather than being limited to the historical generalizations, abstract propositions, and expressions of dismay to which discussions of this subject can all too easily fall prey. The pragmatic emphasis of the conference reflected, as Adrian Marriage so engagingly expressed it, an attempt "to take the subject by indirection and stealth [rather] than by storming it in force."

If we were to have attempted to storm this subject in force, we would have needed to address more explicitly what we mean by liberal education, why we value it, and what manner of dissatisfaction with the present state of affairs in our universities brought us here this weekend. These questions seemed to slosh around in the murky waters of our collective mid-conscious, with comments that responded to them surfacing from time to time and then receding to the hidden shoals which undergirded the waves of case description. Thus, the first question which any summary of this conference which purports to be useful must raise is, "what is the problem for which reform of liberal education curricula is the solution?"

That question immediately gives rise to two subsidiary questions : (i) what are the shortcomings of liberal education in Canadian universities today? (ii) why is it important to rectify these shortcomings? There is a third relevant question which I will address after these two, namely, what are some of the elements which would result in an improvement of liberal education?

SHORTCOMINGS OF LIBERAL EDUCATION AS PRACTISED

Unlike the United States, where there seem to be endless national studies of the state of higher education, some of which apparently have motivated the establishment of the Fund for the Improvement of Postsecondary Education, which Charles Karelis told us about, we have little information on the actual state of liberal education in Canada. Now, given the similarities and the close interaction between higher education in the two nations, there is an ever present tendency to generalize U.S. findings about higher education to our much less studied context. On the other hand, there are major differences between the two nations with respect to structure, traditions, and emphases in higher education, and one can never be sure just which findings about U.S. higher education apply also to us and which do not.[4] Thus, we have no comprehensive studies which inform us as to the applicability here of Allan Bloom's biting indictment of liberal education in the United States:

> It is amazing how many undergraduates are poking around for courses to take, without any plan or question to ask, just filling up their college years... With rare exceptions, the courses are parts of specialities and not designed for general cultivation, or to investigate questions important for human beings as such. The so-called knowledge explosion and increasing specialization have not filled up the college years but emptied them... These great universities — which can split the atom, find cures for the most terrible diseases, conduct surveys of whole populations and produce massive dictionaries of lost languages — cannot generate a modest program of general education for undergraduate students.[5]

Bloom's conclusions about the state of liberal education in the United States in the 1980s would seem, from Charles Karelis's incisive presentation on the subject, to have had considerable impact, even though they are based only upon personal observation and are certainly not new.[6]

From time to time, commentators on the Canadian scene have also raised concerns about the state of liberal education. As long ago as 1967, an observer as circumspect as Robin Harris, in a national conference on the state of Canadian higher education, reported his perception of widespread concern as to "whether the general course offered at Canadian universities can be regarded as adequate."[7]

MICHAEL L. SKOLNIK

Concerns have been raised also in the book that some regard as the Canadian counterpart to Bloom's *The Great Brain Robbery*.[8]

Comments throughout this conference reveal personal observations by a majority of participants that liberal education in Canada suffers from a lack of coherence, direction, vigour, and commitment on the part of their institutions. Of course, it is difficult to generalize from these observations, for this is likely a self-selected group of persons with certain biases about the subject. Indeed, one of the *rapporteurs* remarked that the tenor of the discussion in his workshop was that of a beleaguered minority of voices for liberal education who felt themselves to be crying futilely in the winds of campus indifference. On the other hand, there were a few more optimistic characterizations of things, most notably Howard Clark's comment that on the whole the state of liberal education in Canada was pretty good. In summary, though, I think it's fair to say that the majority of participants felt that — notwithstanding some outstanding examples to the contrary — there is too little emphasis on and support for liberal education in most Canadian universities, and that what is being offered falls well short of what we, collectively as educators, should and could be providing.

Turning to the substantive nature of the voiced concerns about inadequacies of liberal education, the dominant view was that there is too much emphasis on specialization and vocationalism and not enough on breadth and integration in intellectual and personal development. There was some intimation that this is a uniquely late twentieth century problem, because of the high value placed upon specialization and professionalization in our times. It is perhaps useful to counter the latter view — especially in its vocationalism dimension — by noting that the tension between the liberal and the vocational-professional functions of the university has been a major issue in the university for many centuries, and this tension is widely considered to be a source of vitality for the university. It is one thing, however, to appreciate this tension in its historical context, quite another to wax romantically — in contradiction of the evidence — about the university's loss of innocence. From what we know of the first documented universities (like Bologna, Salerno, and to some degree Paris), it would seem that their primary mission was vocational — training for civil and canon law, clergy, and medicine.

When we recall that some early universities became established primarily because students wanted to be taught law or medicine so that they could make a living, there is a curious irony in criticisms of 1980s students for being too career-oriented and lacking interest in knowledge for the sake of knowledge. It has probably always been the case that the vast majority of persons who sought a university education did so primarily with career goals in mind, even if those goals were not too precisely formulated. Having this captive audience, the university has an opportunity to excite wonder and curiosity in larger and deeper questions of purpose and meaning. If we do not see that wonder and

94

curiosity in our students, the fault may not lie in their earlier conditioning or in the heralded crassness of our times, but rather in our failure to kindle the latent passion in most human beings to grapple with those enduring questions of the nature and purpose of life and of the meaning of the world around us. Viewed in this light, vocational motivation is not so much an insurmountable obstacle to liberal education, but a hook that enables us to attract students so that in the process of giving them what they think they want, we can also administer a good dose of what we think they should get.[9]

Specialization was given even more hard knocks during the conference than vocationalism, although it was defended by a minority of participants either for its essentiality to the advancement of knowledge or by humanists in deference to their scientist colleagues. It's fun to criticize over-specialization. My favourite jibe is from Tom Lehrer's song about Werner von Braun : "I send the missiles up, where they come down is someone else's department."

Apart from such quips, the concerns expressed about academic specialization were not about specialization *per se*, but about the way that it impinges upon undergraduate education. I heard a widely endorsed notion that there is at least in theory an integrative experience called liberal education which is antithetical to special-ization and which can be sustained only if somehow insulated from the processes of specialization. Some took pains to emphasize that this insulation need not, could not, and perhaps should not, be total. This is to say, given the importance of specialization in the pursuit of knowledge and in intellectual development, we would be shortchanging our students if we did not give them the experience of working with specialized knowledge. In this I was reminded of the remark attributed to Robert Oppenheimer that the purpose of a university education is twofold: to make the student aware of how much he does not know, and to give him the experience of at least a degree of mastery of some however small body of knowledge.[10]

Viewed thus, the challenge is to strike the right balance between specialized and general knowledge. Even so, there is more here than a problem of curriculum engineering or of resolving conflicting judgments as to what is the right balance. For one thing, the knowledge explosion in the last half of the twentieth century has resulted in a vast and complex proliferation of diverging streams of specialized knowledge. A few centuries ago, maybe even a century ago, it was possible for a person to attain by his early twenties considerable mastery of a particular body of knowledge and at the same time what we would today regard as a strong general education. Leonardo, for example, probably knew everything that was worth knowing about medicine in his time, and could still find time to know much about art, religion, music, history, politics, geography, philosophy, and generally the important ideas of his age. Today a medical scientist can spend a lifetime studying one disease and still feel like she doesn't know all that is known about it.

Insofar as our ideal of liberal education is intertwined with that wonderful idela of the Renaissance man, we would do well to consider whether advances in knowledge have made that ideal anachronistic, or how it might be re-conceptualized in the late twentieth century. In that connection, Lise Bissonnette's notion of "the new classicism" certainly merits more effort at explication than our time constraints permitted. Perhaps somewhat dialectical to that concept, one workshop came up with the phrase "advanced contemporary culture," to provide a framework for its ideas about an approach to liberal education for our time. Both phrases may be seen as metaphors which highlight the particular challenge of extending a classical concept into a contemporary cultural setting, one emphasizing the classical origins and the other, the contemporary setting. And the responsiveness of participants to these and similar expressions of the issue suggested that there was not wide support for a great books curriculum if a necessary condition for "great" would include having been written no later than, say, the eighteenth century. There is an even more fundamental issue in the relationship between specialized and general than volume of knowledge or time perspective, but I will leave that to my comments on obstacles to reform of liberal education.

THE MOTIVATION FOR REFORM OF LIBERAL EDUCATION

Thus far, I have attempted to report the pervasive uneasiness of participants as to whether we are doing a good job of liberal education and corresponding fears that undergraduate curricula may be too dominated by orientations of specialization and vocationalism. Having described this fairly widely held view that there are shortcomings in our approach to liberal education, I am now in a position to address the other leg of the introductory question, "what is the problem for which reform of liberal education is the solution?" Doing so involves reporting on what was said about why liberal education matters.

I was able to distinguish from participants' remarks two major themes of motivation for reform of liberal education. In addition, there is a third, which, possibly because it is to me the most important, I think I heard faintly, or perhaps I projected it.

One of the two major themes was of a purported causal connection between liberal education and ethical behaviour. This theme was prominent in two of the plenary presentations, one of the speakers raising the celebrated case of Ivan Boesky as a metaphor for the decline of public morality in the 1980s, a decline which it was claimed could be reversed by more emphasis on liberal education. Provocative as this metaphor may be, it ignores the fact that Ivan Boeskys have been around as long as commerce itself, to say nothing of politics and public administration, and many of them have been liberally educated. The treachery of Anthony Blunt, for example, a model of the liberally educated person, exceeded Boesky's abuse of inside information by a wide margin. The assertion that liberal education produces a higher level of ethical behaviour may be an excessive claim, or at least one which we, as social scientists, should be more careful in making, without supporting evidence, if we are concerned about our credibility both as educators and scientists.

A related argument on behalf of liberal education is that which emphasizes the importance of liberal education for those who will assume positions of power with respect to technology, particularly nuclear technology, and the tools of war. The loose version of this argument postulates an association between liberal education and peace-making, or at least reduction of the arms race. This argument flies in the face of historical evidence of the role of liberally educated persons in starting wars, and, worse, committing atrocities, Goebbels, as someone noted, being a case in point. On the other hand, three decades after C.P. Snow warned of the dangers of the split between scientific and humanistic cultures, this is as serious a problem as ever. Temperate statements of the importance of bridging this gap in the hope that those in charge of technology will be more sensitive to the social and human impacts of technology would seem to provide a plausible rationale for ensuring a liberal component in the training of scientists. In this connection, many participants noted that science students are far more likely to be exposed to the humanities than vice-versa.

The other major argument presented on behalf of liberal education, also instrumental, related to what I would term its "vocational" benefits. It has in recent years become almost commonplace to hear employers complain that recent graduates are lacking in such qualities as flexibility, adaptability, creativity, analytical skills, and the ability to communicate well orally and in writting. We heard an eloquent statement of this perception from Jon Grant. And such reports from employers have been mirrored somewhat in research findings in the Economics of Education. In a subset of that literature which addresses what has been called "the screening hypothesis" (or sometimes "credentialism"), one prominent commentator has observed that most jobs in a modern industrial economy can be learned on the job in a relatively short time by one who has a good general education *and* the apporpritate non-cognitive traits.[11]

The implication of these expressions of employers' dissatisfaction with new graduates together with research findings about the screening hypothesis is that graduate with liberal (or general — rarely is a distinction made between the two) education might be more productive in many jobs than graduates from more occupationally specific programs. However, the evidential base for this conclusion is somewhat fragile. Employers who have made this argument seem to assume that since skills that they seek are of a generic type and since they're not getting people with those skills from specialized programs, they would get the desired skills from graduates of programs which were more general or liberal.[12] Among Economics of Education researchers, opinion is divided as to whether general education programs do, or could, inculcate the desired generic skills; or whether these skills are formed elsewhere than schools, and educational institutions merely screen for them and certify their presence. Thus, while it is fashionable to attribute alleged shortcomings of graduates with respect to such qualities as adaptability and analytical ability to overspecialization of curricula, and to assume that a more general curriculum would remedy the shortcomings, there is not a great deal of empirical support for this assertion. Perhaps that is why even in the company of which Mr. Grant is President, he acknowledges that the personnel manager continues to hire graduates on the basis of their occupationally specific education.

Another issue that arises in conjunction with justifying liberal education in terms of its purported vocational outcomes relates to curriculum. The vocational rationale for liberal education leads to what Professor Marriage described as "the fashionable view that it has no subject matter at all;" it is concerned merely with the imparting of abstract skills. Having courses which attempt explicitly to develop particular skills that are desired by employers may be a quite useful and appropriate activity for the university, but many would argue that this is not what liberal education is. One might argue, for example, that quite independently of what the university provides in the way of liberal education, it should ensure that *all* of its graduates possess adequate analytical and communications skills.

Perhaps it was because the conference shied away from defining liberal education that the more fundamental, age-old rationale for liberal education did not surface explicitly much during the conference, though a number of comments seemed to be rooted implicitly in this rationale. This is the view that liberal education, as Australian educator Geoffrey Partington expresses it, "is defined by its central concern with the development of the mind by initiation into knowledge deemed to be intrinsically valuable (and independent of the demands of any particular trade or profession), and by its adherence to some notion of hierarchy within knowledge.[13] It is these notions of intrinsically valuable knowledge and hierarchy (that is to say, some knowledge is more worth having than other) that Bloom has in mind when he says that "the university must stand for something."

Possibly, due to the association of the ideas about liberal education of Plato or Newman or T.S. Eliot (or Bloom) with elitist preparation for leaders, we have become self-conscious about the classical ideal of liberal education. Yet, as Partington notes, even in traditional socialist thought there is a powerful strand that the best of culture should be the inheritance of the many, not just the few. Partington quotes Thomas Burt, the first Labour member of the British House of Commons: "Educate a man not simply because he has political power and simply to make him a good workman; but educate him because he is a man."

In the conference, this rationale for liberal education foundered on the shoals of relativism as well as those of elitism. Bloom's book and

Karelis' lecture both described well how relativism (particularly in its view that all cultural knowledge is equally worthwhile) has sapped the lifeblood of liberal education, and this argument need not be repeated here. There was a strong disinclination in most of the workshops to say what liberal education is and why it's important, apart from the type of vague ethical and vocational claims noted above. Rather, the tendency was to say that liberal education can be many different things to different people, and so long as those different people find something useful to them in their concept, they should have the support to develop an approach to it that is consistent with their concept of liberal education. An exception was Jon Grant, in his remark that the university must be a beacon in a world constantly buffeted by transient influences, something that can give people rooting and the capacity to critically evaluate such influences. Without any solid consensus as to what liberal education is or willingness to take a stand on its intrinsic merit, it is not surprising that liberal education should be in the state of disarray that many participants felt it to be. There was much discussion of obstacles to the improvement of liberal education — to which I turn next — but possibly the greatest problem is not the obstacles along our path, but that we don't know where we would want to go even if those obstacles weren't in the way.

OBSTACLES TO THE ADVANCEMENT OF LIBERAL EDUCATION

We heard a lot about obstacles to liberal education - so much in fact that one participant remarked that the most depressing thing about the conference was learning of obstacles that he hadn't thought of before. We were given some nice classifications of obstacles: organizational, pedagogical, political, financial, managerial, cultural, professional and so on. But, in my view, the paradigmatic obstacle described by Adrian Marriage is the fundamental one, and all the others are symptoms or reflections of it.

This fundamental obstacle is that the dominant view of knowledge in the university is that the only legitimate knowledge (that is, not "popular" or "journalistic") is that produced through the division of intellectual labour among (and increasingly within) the academic disciplines. This view is the legacy of what Jencks and Riesman described as the Academic Revolution: a process which has involved a shift from teaching to research as the primary focus of the university and the emergence of research-preoccupied disciplinary communities as the arbiters of institutional priorities and values.[14] These disciplinary communities conceptualize knowledge in terms of a set of data, theories, and methodologies which facilitate advancement of the discipline. This paradigm of knowledge has major implications for the structure and conduct of the academic enterprise; for example, the university reward system encourages activities which foster the advancement of disciplinary knowledge and discourage those which do not.

The problem for liberal education, as Professor Marriage argues, is that it is inherently integrative — in the limiting case aiming for the unity of knowledge, as Peter Morgan put it — or at least indifferent to disciplinary boundaries, and hence it doesn't appear on our map of knowledge. It's not that liberal education is explicitly rejected or opposed, though in some quarters it might be dismissed as an anachronism; it's that we can't get there using our map of knowledge. Here again, it's unfortunate that the conference didn't try harder to explicate the concept of liberal education, but from the modest efforts that were made it was clear that what most of us meant by liberal education was something that cannot be located within a disciplinary rubric. In short — and this observation deserves more elaboration than I can give it here — liberal education seems to be rooted in a different paradigm of knowledge than the dominant one on which the contemporary university is based.

This discomfiture of liberal education with the dominant paradigm of knowledge in the university gives rise to an awkward question, namely, was Cardinal Newman right in his view of the incompatibility of teaching and research? Now, higher educators, in their presidential or commencement addresses, love to quote Newman, thereby reinforcing the connection between the contemporary university and its historic precursors. However, one major theme of Newman's which they don't like to talk about — except to show how even the ideas of a great thinker have been superseded by the advances of modernity — is the Cardinal's view of the university as preeminently "a place of teaching universal knowledge... not of scientific and philosophical discovery."[15] Newman's statements on teaching and research focused primarily on human nature, a construct which has fallen into some disrepute (but which nevertheless should probably be discussed in a good liberal arts program) : "to discover and teach are distinct functions; they are also distinct gifts, and are not commonly found united in the same person... the greatest thinkers have been too intent upon their subject to admit of interruption."

Marriage's observations about maps of knowledge implies a somewhat different basis for the incompatibility between teaching and research, though it is probably one which Newman appreciated, as he was witness to the development of academic specialization. The contemporary paradigm of knowledge in the university is research-driven and is well suited to advancing research, professional training, and graduate studies in most (but not necessarily all)[16] subject fields. But it is arguable whether this research-driven paradigm facilitates undergraduate liberal education, and it is in that sense that there may be a fundamental conflict between teaching and research. Courses which are designed to be part of a liberal education are different from courses which are designed to be part of a hierarchical sequence within a discipline, and liberal education is something different in a liberal arts college that is uninvolved in research and graduate studies from what it is in a research university.[17]

LEARNING FROM OUR EXPERIENCE

Canada doesn't have any liberal arts colleges equivalent to Oberlin, Reed, Pomona, Sarah Lawrence and so many others in the United States, so we have to work within the framework of the comprehensive research university. It may well be that the price we have to pay for the particular structure of higher education that we have chosen is weakness, or at least, fragility of liberal education.[18] In that connection, it was interesting that those who felt most satisfied with liberal education on their campus were in programs which are to a considerable degree insulated from the rest of the campus, for example, British Columbia, Concordia, and McMaster. Of course, it may be possible to negotiate such insulation only where the liberal education program is a relatively small portion of the student's total under-graduate experience, for example the equivalent of 9 credit hours in the UBC Arts One Program — but this is regarded as definitely better than nothing. Similarly, the programs seem more likely to be acceptable where they enrol a small minority of students, and we heard an eloquent expression of concern from a McMaster professor about not reaching more students. Possibly, as word gets around the student body and more students ask for these innovative liberal education programs, additional resources will be allocated to them in order to serve larger numbers of students. On the other hand, too much visibility could place these programs in jeopardy.

A second conclusion is that while some combinations of existing courses are probably better than others for purposes of enhancing liberal education, the simple manipulation of those building blocks — through electives or prescribed sets —— is of quite limited value because few existing courses within disciplines are designed for the general cultivation of students. Rather, there was a feeling that, at minimum, there should be new courses deliberately designed to provide a different type of learning experience from the courses which are intended to provide specialist training (or prepare students for the next level course within a discipline). Ideally, these new courses should constitute an integrated whole, as in the proposed program at the University of Toronto.

The idea of providing new courses as electives to be added to the patchwork of existing courses suffers from the problems outlined by Dr. Karelis in his comments on curricular reform at Harvard.[19] The curriculum reform at Harvard was achieved only through a decade of seemingly endless committee meetings, position papers, and draft proposals, culminating in what some have described as "a glorious delicatessen," and what Dr. Karelis described as "core-light." Though the descriptions of the new courses which Keller provides would seem to offer many fascinating possibilities (an examination of the creative process by examining how artists like Beethoven and Shakespeare resolved the artistic and philosophical problems with which they wrestled through a lifetime of creativity; or a study of renaissances and revivals in different countries and different times, comparing causes, characteristics, effects, and relationships with pertinent social and political conditions), some have wondered whether the modest achievement was worth the effort, the process of curricular reform being likened to "moving a cemetery." Still, where the development of a whole program is not feasible, some will find adding new courses a worthwhile, if second best, solution.

A third conclusion is that reform of liberal education should be seen not just as of benefit to students, but as a potentially valuable exercise in institutional self-reflection and renewal, particularly as a means for rejuvenating faculty in this era of concern with aging and burn-out. Several participants spoke of the benefits for faculty of engaging in dialogue with colleagues about what it means to be an educated person in the late twentieth century, and rolling up their sleeves to develop (or in the case of UBC Arts One, re-develop) a program which merits the name "new classicism," "advanced contemporary culture," or the like. No doubt, this experience is not for everyone, but enabling those who would respond to the opportunity (including those who have lost, at least temporarily, the urge to do research) could be an important part of a university's renewal strategy. Further, this experience, and the inherent focus on teaching, might have spillover benefits with regard to improving of teaching when these faculty go back to their discipline courses, assuming that, as at UBC, the participation in these programs is on a rotational basis.

Finally, I should like to return to the issue of whether innovative liberal education programs like those of UBC, Concordia, and McMaster should be for all students. This was an item of concern in all workshops. On the one hand, there was a feeling that it was important to make this opportunity available to all students because it could be such a good experience and because to do otherwise *would* be elitist. On the other hand, there was a recognition that some students might not want this type of opportunity, for example, because they know what they want to specialize in and they want to get on with it; and there was little inclination to force students to take such a program.

The challenge is to create the type of liberal education program which students would see as too exciting an opportunity to pass up. Lack of student interest in liberal education to date might be seen to be a rational reaction to choices with which students have been presented and the insipid way that liberal education has often been presented in contrast to the glamour of specialization. If those who urge the intrinsic worth of liberal education are correct in their view that there beats within the hearts of many, if not most, humans a deep longing to partake in a dialogue of primeval origin about the pervasive questions of life which have historically been at the core of liberal education and arise in challenging forms in the late twentieth century, then it is imperative for the university to find the ingenuity, the time, and the resources to initiate students into that dialogue. Few things could be more central to the mission of the university.

MICHAEL L. SKOLNIK

NOTES

1. This paper is an edited (and documented) version of the summary observations and comments which the author presented at the conclusion of the Conference "Who's Afraid of Liberal Education?"

2. *The Methodology of the Social Sciences* (Glencoe : The Free Press, 1949), p. 269. I have wrestled with the somewhat unique blurring of the subject-object distinction for the academic who specializes in research on higher education where he himself is a participant in the enterprise which he studies. See "Role Conflicts of a Professor of Higher Education : An Autobiographical Case Study," in W. Shere and R. Duhamel, eds. *Academic Futures : Prospects for Postsecondary Education* (Toronto : OISE Press, 1987), pp. 108-127.

3. *The Mission of the University* (Princeton University : Princeton University Press, 1944).

4. For a concise discussion of differences between university systems in the two countries, see Peter Leslie, *Canadian Universities 1980 and Beyond: Enrolment, Structural Change, and Finance* (Ottawa : Association of Universities and Colleges of Canada, 1980), pp. 56-65. I have attempted to treat this subject in more detail in "Diversity in Higher Education: The Canadian Case," *Higher Education in Europ* 11, 2 (1986), pp. 19-32.

5. *The Closing of the American Mind* (New York : Simon and Schuster, 1987), p. 340. In the context in which the above quote is presented, the distinction between liberal and general education is not at issue though in other contexts it might well be.

6. Writing about the reforms of undergraduate education at Harvard under President Lowell in the early twentieth century, after the move to electives under Eliot in the late nineteenth, historian Samuel Morrison remarked, "Lowell... put back into the academic basket some of the things that had fallen through the mesh during the process of expansion [under Eliot]. Of these, the most important was education." Quoted in Phyllis Keller, *Getting at the Core : Curricular Reform at Harvard* (Cambridge : Harvard University Press, 1982), p. 10. Apparently there was a feeling that some things had again fallen through the mesh by the 1970s, giving rise to the curricular reform initiative which Keller's fascinating book documents.

7. "A Matter of Balance," in Association of Universities and Colleges of Canada, *Proceedings of National Conference, 1967* (Ottawa : AUCC, 1967), p. 19.

8. D. Bercuson, R. Bothwell, and J.L. Granatstein (Toronto : McClelland and Stewart, 1984). The critique provided by these authors, while more pragmatic and less comprehensive than Bloom's, zeroes in on what they regard as undue specialization at the undergraduate level.

9. This hook argument is a variant of what some view as the university's Faustian Bargain with a society which does not fully appreciate or accept the non-utilitarian objectives of the university. In this view, the university devotes some of its energy to providing what society claims to want, in return for which the university is given resources and left alone to do the things that it regards as important. So long as the balance in this exchange is not too one-sided, each party accepts that it cannot have all of what it wants and there is an equilibrium. Crises occur when the university comes to feel that it is asked to become too much a hand-maiden of the state, or when politicians come to feel that the university has been allowed to become too much of an ivory tower, the latter depicting the current state of affairs in the United Kingdom, and perhaps the recent situation in British Columbia; the former a situation which many professors feel is developing in Ontario.

10. I am indebted to my colleague in the Higher Education Group, Ian Winchester, for this and a few other examples used in this paper. For an excellent discussion of the issues involved in reconciling the liberal role of the university with the pressures toward specialization arising in the contemporary age of science, see his article "The Future of a Mediaeval Institution : the University in the Twenty-first Century." in W.A.W. Nielson and C. Gaffield, eds., *Universities in Crisis: A Mediaeval Institution in the Twenty-first Century* (Montreal : The Institute for Research on Public Policy, 1986), pp. 231-250.

11. Mark Blaug, "Where are We Now in the Economics of Education," *Economics of Education Review* 4, 1 (1985), pp. 17-28.

12. It is interesting to note that while on this side of the Atlantic one hears arguments that more emphasis on liberal education would be good for business, just the opposite is taking place in the United Kingdom. Noel Annan writes in the *New York Review* (September 29, 1988) about the concern that obsession with the cultural ideals of Newman and Arnold has deprived British industry of the skills and entrepreneurial zeal needed to make the U.K. a first-rate economic power and that the purpose of the Thatcher government's attack on the universities is to corral that intellectutal horse and make it "haul carts rather than gallop over Newmarket Heath."

13. "The Disorientation of Western Education," *Encounter* (January, 1987), p. 14.

14. C. Jencks and D. Riesman, *The Academic Revolution* (Chicago : University of Chicago Press, 1977).

15. John Henry Newman, *On the Scope and Nature of University Education* (London : J.M. Dent and Sons Ltd., 1915), p. xxix.

16. Its appropriateness for the natural and applied sciences is indisputable. Bloom questions whether it facilitates work in the humanities, and Donald Schon questions whether it facilitates training in some professions — *The Reflective Practitioner: How Professionals Think in Action* (New York : Basic Books, Inc., 1982).

17. Charles Karelis reported that liberal arts is generally in a healthier state in Catholic universities, even large ones, than in secular universities. This suggests that where there is sufficient conviction and will to, in Bloom's words, take a stand, this paradigmatic obstacle might be overcome, at least to some degree. It is doubtful, however, whether in the absence of a unifying force such as that which religion can provide, the paradigmatic obstacle can be overcome within a comprehensive university. For an interesting discussion of the difference that a religious frame of reference can make to liberal education, see Christopher Derrick, *Escape from Skepticism : Liberal Education as if Truth Mattered* (Peru, Illinois : Sherwood Sugden & Company, Fourth Printing, 1987).

18. On this structural difference between Canadian and U.S. higher education, see the references in note 4.

19. See also Keller (note 6).

CAROLINE ANDREW

Caroline Andrew is president of the Social Science Federation of Canada for the year 1988-89. She is a professor in the Department of Political Science at the University of Ottawa and Vice-Dean of the Faculty of Social Sciences.

LISE BISSONNETTE

Following her graduate studies in Education, Lise Bissonnette has had an impressive journalism career : columnist on education issues for *Le Devoir* and then parliamentary correspondent in Quebec City and in Ottawa. From 1978 to 1985 she was editorialist and Assistant Editor in Chief, then Editor in Chief with Le Devoir. Since 1985, Lise Bissonnette has been a regular columnist with the *Globe and Mail, le Soleil*, and *l'Actualité*. Moreover, she is special advisor on Quebec and Canadian Affairs for the Charles R. Bronfman Foundation and has recently agreed to host a weekly television broadcast with Radio-Québec. She is frequently invited to speak on Quebec political and cultural issues in various universities both in Canada and in the United States.

HOWARD C. CLARK

Dr. Clark assumed the position of President and Vice-Chancellor of Dalhousie University in September, 1986. Dr. Clark came to Dalhousie after a ten-year term as Vice-President, Academic at the University of Guelph. Prior to that he held teaching and administrative positions at the University of Western Ontario, the University of British Columbia and Auckland University. A New Zealand native, Dr. Clark was educated at the University of New Zealand and Cambridge. Dr. Clark's academic interests lie in the field of chemistry; he has published over 240 papers and remains actively involved in research. He is a Fellow of the Royal Society of Canada, a past President of the Chemical Institute of Canada, and has received a number of other awards and honours in the field of chemistry.

STEEN B. ESBENSEN

Dr. Esbensen assumed the position of Executive Director of the Social Science Federation of Canada in 1988. He came to the Federation on leave from the Université du Québec à Hull where he was Director of the Ph.D in Education program and professor of early childhood education (1978-1988). He has taught at Quinsigamond Community College, Worcester, Massachusetts, (1973-1974) the Université de Moncton, (1976-1977), the University of British Columbia (1980 and 1981) and served the Canadian Society for the Study of Education as Executive Director (1982-1988). Esbensen was educated at Tufts University and the University of Massachusetts, Amherst. His academic interests have focused on teacher education, learning environments and children's rights. He has authored numerous books and articles and delivered many papers and presentations on issues related to his academic interests. His interest in Liberal Arts Undergraduate Education has been strongly influenced by the Tufts experience with the College Within and program development in teacher education while at UQAH.

JON K. GRANT

Jon K. Grant, President and Chief Executive Officer of the Quaker Oats Comsany of Canada, is a graduate of the School of Business Administration of the University of Western Ontario. Mr. Grant is a Member of the Advisory Committee of the School of Business Administration of the University of Western Ontario, the Agricultural Council of Ontario, the Business Council on National Issues, and the Corporate Higher Education Forum. He has spoken widely on issues facing the food industry and the role of Trustees in public institutions.

CLAUDE HAMEL

Claude Hamel assumed the position of President of the Université du Québec in September 1988. He came to the Université du Québec in 1985 as Vice-President, Academic. Prior to that he held teaching and administrative positions at the Université de Sherbrooke, Vice-President, Administration (1975-1981), and President, (1981-1985). A native of Victoriaville, Québec, Claude Hamel was educated at the Séminaire de Sherbrooke, B.A. (1954), the Université de Sherbrooke,

B.Sc.A. (1959) and Laval M.Sc.A. (1964). He is a member of numerous provincial and national councils, commissions, adjudication committees and task forces concerning university and academic affairs. He is a member of the Ordre des ingénieurs du Québec (CREPUQ), of the Association of Universities and Colleges of Canada and of the Association des universités partiellement ou entièrement de langue française (AUPELF).

CHARLES KARELIS

Charles Karelis, who holds a Ph.D from Oxford University, teaches at Williams College and Wesleyan University. In 1985, he held the position of Special Assistant to the U.S. Secretary of Education, and the same year was appointed Director of the Fund for the Improvement of Post-secondary Education of the U.S. Department of Education. He has published two books and numerous articles, and has given many papers on various issues related to education.

ADRIAN MARRIAGE

Mr. Adrian Marriage is a graduate of the London School of Economics and is presently a professor of Sociology and Chair of the Arts I Programme at the University of British Columbia. Author of numerous studies in criminology and on the Canadian judiciary system, Mr. Marriage has held many administrative positions in his Department and Faculty, and he holds membership in a number of professional and government associations (B.C. Civil Liberties Association; Canadian Mental Health Association, etc.).

PETER MORGAN

Peter Morgan is an expert in the field of 19th century literature and is also interested in the relations between literature and the visual arts. A professor at the University of Toronto since 1960, Peter Morgan obtained his B.A. from the University of Birmingham, his M.A. and Ph.D. from the University of London. He has published numerous articles and book reviews, and is the author or editor of more than a half a dozen books. He has worked on many study programme committees and is presently responsible for the implementation of an integrated curriculum programme.

GILLES PAQUET

Gilles Paquet is Professor of Economics and Public management at the Faculty of Administration, University of Ottawa. A native of Quebec city, Dr. Paquet received his undergraduate training in philosophy and social sciences at Laval University. He did his graduate work in economics at Laval and Queen's University and was a post-doctoral scholar in economics at the University of California. Professor of Economics at Carleton University (1963-1981); Dean of Graduate Studies and Research at Carleton University (1973-1979); Dean of the Faculty of Administration at the University of Ottawa (1981-1988); Scholar-in-

CONTRIBUTORS

Residence at the Institute for Research on Public Policy (1988-1989). Dr. Paquet holds many positions in scholarly associations (Canadian Economic Association; Société canadienne de science économique) and in a number of national organizations (President of the Social Sciences Federation of Canada, 1981-1982; Secretary-Treasurer of the Royal Society since 1983; President of ACFAS, 1986-1987). He is also consultant to a number of agencies and ministries and host/journalist of a weekly economic affairs magazine at Radio-Canada. Dr. Paquet authored/co-authored six books and some 70 papers and chapters in edited books on issues in economic history, regional development, regulation of socio-economic systems and public administration.

MICHAEL L. SKOLNIK

Dr. Skolnik is a professor of higher education at the Ontario Institute for Studies in Education and at the graduate department of education at the University of Toronto. A Rhodes Scholar who studied at Oxford University, he also did graduate work at Berkeley during the infamous period of the sixties. Dr. Skolnik has published a number of books and papers on issues related to higher education, including, "Please sir, I want some more : Canadian universities under financial restraint"; "The Shell Game called System Rationalization" (*Higher Education*); "If the cut is so deep, where is the blood?" (*Review of Higher Education*); "Role conflicts in the professional study of Higher Education" (*Academic Futures*); "How academic program review can foster intellectual conformity and stifle creativity in the University" (forthcoming in the *Journal of Higher Education*); "Diversity in Higher Education; the Canadian Case" (*European Review of Higher Education*).

LES COLLABORATEURS

CAROLINE ANDREW

Caroline Andrew est présidente de la Fédération canadienne des sciences sociales pour l'année 1988-89. Elle est professeure au Département de science politique à l'Université d'Ottawa et Vice-doyenne de la Faculté des sciences sociales.

LISE BISSONNETTE

Après des études supérieures en éducation, Lise Bissonnette a connu une brillante carrière journalistique : chroniqueur d'éducation au Devoir, puis correspondante parlementaire à Québec et à Ottawa, elle occupe, de 1978 à 1985, les fonctions d'éditorialiste et rédactrice en chef adjointe, puis de rédactrice en chef du *Devoir*. Depuis 1985, Lise Bissonnette écrit régulièrement des chroniques pour le *Globe and Mail*, le *Soleil*, l'*Actualité*. Elle est en outre responsable des affaires canadiennes et québécoises à la Fondation Charles R. Bronfman et, récemment, elle a accepté une émission de télévision hebdomadaire à Radio-Québec. Elle est fréquemment invitée à parler sur la politique et la culture québécoise dans diverses universités, tant au Canada qu'au États-Unis.

HOWARD C. CLARK

M. Clark est président et vice-chancelier de l'université Dalhousie depuis septembre 1986. Il avait auparavant occupé les fonctions de vice-président, enseignement et recherche à l'Université de Guelph pendant dix ans. Il a également occupé des fonctions d'enseignement et divers postes administratifs aux universités de Western Ontario, de Colombie-Britannique et d'Auckland. Né en Nouvelle-Zélande, M. Clark a fait ses études aux universités de Nouvelle-Zélande et de Cambridge. Son champ de spécialisation est la chimie; il a publié plus de deux cent quarante articles, et il demeure actif en recherche. Titulaire de nombreuses distinctions et décorations, M. Clark est membre de la Société royale du Canada et président sortant de l'Institut de chimie du Canada.

STEEN B. ESBENSEN

M. Steen Esbensen détient le poste de directeur général de la Fédération canadienne des sciences sociales depuis 1988. Il est en congé de l'Université du Québec à Hull où il dirigeait le programme de doctorat en éducation et enseignait dans le domaine de l'éducation préscolaire (1978-1988). Il a également enseigné au Quinsigamond Community College à Worcester au Massachusetts (1973-1974), à l'Université de Moncton (1976-1977), à l'University of British-Columbia (1980 et 1981) et a agi à titre de directeur général de la Société canadienne pour l'étude de l'éducation (1982-1988). Le professeur Esbensen a étudié à la Tufts University et à l'University of Massachusetts à Amherst. Il s'intéresse principalement à la formation des enseignants, à l'environnement d'apprentissage et aux droits des enfants. Il est l'auteur de nombreux ouvrages et articles et il a prononcé plusieurs conférences. Ce sont surtout ses expériences vécues au College Within de la Tufts University et à l'Université du Québec à Hull qui l'ont amené à s'intéresser plus sérieusement à la question de l'éducation générale.

JON K. GRANT

Président et directeur général de la compagnie Quaker Oats du Canada, M. Grant est diplômé en administration des affaires de l'université Western Ontario. Il est membre du comité aviseur de la School of Business administration de l'université Western Ontario, du Agricultural Council of Ontario, du Conseil canadien des chefs d'entreprises et du forum Université-Entreprise. Il a prononcé de nombreuses conférences sur l'industrie agro-alimentaire et sur le rôle des administrateurs dans les institutions publiques.

CLAUDE HAMEL

Claude Hamel est natif de Victoriaville au Québec. Il a fait ses études au Séminaire de Sherbrooke et obtenu un baccalauréat ès arts (B.A.) en 1954. Il a poursuivi ses études à l'Université de Sherbrooke qui lui a décerné un baccalauréat ès sciences appliquées (B.Sc.A) en 1959. Il a ensuite obtenu une maîtrise ès sciences appliquées (M.Sc.A.) de l'Université Laval in 1964. De 1960 à 1985, Claude Hamel est à l'emploi de l'Université de Sherbrooke où il occupe des fonctions d'enseignement, de recherche et de gestion. De 1975 à 1981, il est vice-recteur à l'administration et de 1981 à 1985 il est recteur. En 1985, il devient vice-président à l'enseignement et à la recherche de l'Université du Québec. En septembre 1988, le gouvernement du Québec le nomme Président de l'Université. Claude Hamel est membre tant à l'interne qu'au niveau québécois et canadien, de multiples conseils, commissions, jurys et comités touchant les affaires universitaires. Il est notamment membre de l'Ordre des ingénieurs du Québec, de la Conférence des recteurs et des principaux des universités du Québec (CREPUQ), de l'Association des universités et collèges du Canada (AUCC) et de l'Association des universités partiellement ou entièrement de langue française (AUPELF).

CHARLES KARELIS

Détenteur d'un doctorat en philosophie de l'université d'Oxford, Charles Karelis a enseigné à Williams College et à la Wesleyan University. En 1985, il acceptait un poste d'adjoint spécial auprès du ministre de l'Éducation et, la même année, il était nommé directeur du Fund for the Improvement of Post-Secondary Education. Il a publié deux livres et de nombreux articles, et il a prononcé de nombreuses conférences sur divers sujets touchant au domaine de l'éducation.

ADRIAN MARRIAGE

Diplômé en sociologie de la London School of Economics, Adrian Marriage est présentement professeur de sociologie et directeur du programme "Arts I" de l'université de Colombie-Britannique. Auteur de nombreux ouvrages sur la criminologie et le système judiciaire canadien, M. Marriage a occupé de nombreuses fonctions administratives au sein de son département et de sa faculté, et il est membre de nombreuses associations professionnelles et gouvernmentales (B.C. Civil Liberties Association; Canadian Mental Health Association, etc.).

PETER MORGAN

Peter Morgan est un spécialiste de la littérature du XIXe siècle et il s'intéresse aux relations entre la littérature et les arts visuels. Professeur à l'université de Toronto depuis 1960, Peter Morgan a obtenu un B.A. de l'université de Birmingham, une maîtrise et un Ph.D. de l'université de Londres. Il a publié de nombreux articles et recensions de livres, en plus d'avoir publié ou édité plus d'une demi-douzaine de livres. Il a participé à plusieurs comités d'étude des programmes et il est présentement responsable de l'élaboration d'un projet de curriculum intégré.

GILLES PAQUET

Gilles Paquet est professeur de science économique et management public à la Faculté d'administration de l'Université d'Ottawa. Né à Québec, M. Paquet a fait ses études de premier cycle en philosophie et en sciences sociales à l'Université Laval et ses études supérieures

LES COLLABORATEURS

en économique à Laval et à l'université Queen's. Il a fait un stage post-doctoral à l'université de Californie. De 1963 à 1981, il a enseigné l'économique à l'Université Carleton, où il a aussi occupé le poste de doyen des études avancées et de la recherche de 1973 à 1979. De 1981 à 1988, il a été doyen de la Faculté d'administration de l'Université d'Ottawa. Pendant l'année 1988-1989, il est chercheur invité à l'Institut de recherches politiques. Il a occupé de nombreuses fonctions au sein d'associations professionnelles (Association canadienne d'économique, Société canadienne de science économique) et d'organisations nationales (président de la Fédération canadienne des sciences sociales, 1981-1982; secrétaire-trésorier de la Société royale du Canada depuis 1983; président de l'ACFAS, 1986-1987). Il est en outre consultant pour plusieurs agences et ministères et il est animateur/journaliste à une émission hebdomadaire d'affaires économiques à Radio-Canada depuis 1978. M. Paquet a publié six livres et plus de 70 articles et chapitres de livres en histoire économique, développement régional et administration publique.

MICHAEL L. SKOLNIK
M. Skolnik est professeur d'éducation à l'Institut d'étude en éducation de l'Ontario et au département d'éducation de l'université de Toronto. Boursier Rhodes, il a étudié à l'université d'Oxford et il a fait des études supérieures à l'université Berkeley pendant les années 60. M. Skolnik a publié de nombreux livres et articles dans le domaine de l'éducation supérieure. Signalons : "Please sir, I want some more : Canadian universities under financial restraint"; "The Shell Game called System Rationalization" (*Higher Education*); "If the cut is so deep, where is the blood?" (*Review of Higher Education*); "Role conflicts in the professional study of Higher Education" (*Academic Futures*); "How academic program review can foster intellectual conformity and stifle creativity in the university" (forthcoming in the *Journal of Higher Education*); "Diversity in Higher Education : the Canadian Case" (*European Review of Higher Education*).